WITHDRAWN

Primary Education
from
Plowden to the 1990s

School Development and the Management of Change Series

Series Editors: Peter Holly and Geoff Southworth
Cambridge Institute of Education
Cambridge, CB2 2BX, UK

School Development and the Management of Change Series: 4

Primary Education
from
Plowden to the 1990s

Norman Thomas

The Falmer Press
(A member of the Taylor & Francis Group)
London • New York • Philadelphia

UK   The Falmer Press, Rankine Road, Basingstoke, Hampshire RG24 0PR

USA   The Falmer Press, Taylor & Francis Inc., 1900 Frost Road, Suite 101, Bristol, PA 19007

First published 1990

British Library Cataloguing in Publication Data
Thomas, Norman 1921
   Primary education from Plowden to the 1990's. (School development and the management of change series; 4)
   1. England. Primary education, history
   I. Title   II. Series
   372.942

   ISBN 1-85000-708-X
   ISBN 1-85000-709-8 pbk

Library of Congress Cataloging-in-Publication Data are available on request

Typeset in 12/14 Garamond by
Chapterhouse, The Cloisters, Formby L37 3PX

Jacket design by Caroline Archer

Printed in Great Britain by Taylor & Francis (Printers) Ltd, Basingstoke on paper which has a specified pH value on final paper manufacture of not less than 7.5 and is therefore 'acid free'.

Contents

Acknowledgments

This book owes a great debt to the thousands of children, teachers and inspectors that I have had the privilege to work with. In particular, it would not have been produced without the patience of my wife, the helpful comments on the text by Derek Willmer, Jill Singer and Geoff Southworth, and Paul Thomas' help in unravelling the computer.

My thanks are due to the Controller of Her Majesty's Stationery Office for permission to reproduce extracts from HMSO publications listed.

List of Abbreviations

ACSET	Advisory Council for the Supply and Education of Teachers
APU	Assessment of Performance Unit, formerly a Unit in the Department of Education and Science and now part of the School Examinations and Assessment Council
ASE	Association for Science Education
ATM	Association of Teachers of Mathematics
CBI	Confederation of British Industry
DENI	Department of Education of Northern Ireland
DES	Department of Education and Science
HMI	Her Majesty's Inspectorate (or Inspector) of Schools
ILEA	Inner London Education Authority
IQ	Intelligence Quotient
LA	Local Authority, some of which include a Local Education Authority
LEA	Local Education Authority, all of which, except the ILEA, are part of a Local Authority
LEATGS	Local Education Authority Training Grants Scheme, through which Central Government Funds are distributed mainly for teachers' in-service education
MA	Mathematical Association
NATE	National Association for the Teaching of English
NCC	National Curriculum Council, set up under the 1988 Education Reform Act and concerned with the whole curriculum in schools, including the National Curriculum

NFER	National Foundation for Educational Research
NS6	A reading test used in national surveys of reading ability between 1955 and the late 1970s
SACRE	Standing Advisory Council in Religious Education, to be set up by each Local Education Authority under the 1988 Education Reform Act
SATS	Standardised Assessment Tasks, to be devised to contribute to the assessment of children's progress at the ends of the Key Stages (ie at about ages 7, 11, 14 and 16) in the National Curriculum
SEAC	School Examinations and Assessment Council, set up under the 1988 Education Reform Act to oversee the schools public examination system and testing and assessment under the National Curriculum
SCDC	Schools Curriculum Development Committee, responsible for projects aimed at developing the curriculum, now replaced by the National Curriculum Council
TA	Teachers' Assessments of children's performance in the National Curriculum, which may be modified by the results obtained in the Standardised Assessment Tasks
TGAT	Task Group on Assessment and Testing, one of the short lived working groups set up by the Secretary of State for Education and Science in preparation for the National Curriculum
TUC	Trades Union Congress
WO	Welsh Office

Introduction

This book is a reflection on some of the changes that have taken place in primary education over the last twenty years or so and that are likely to take place during the next few years. For the most part, the changes considered are those touching on the curriculum and methodology. Some important developments, like the changing relations between schools and parents, the changing roles of governing bodies and the local management of schools are considered only in passing.

In the day-to-day life of a school, immediate issues are pressing and it can be difficult to set incidents and changes in their context. This has particularly been so in the last two years or so, when a mass of material has poured through school letterboxes, a lot of it requiring, or seeming to require, quick action. I hope that this book will remind its readers of the origins and contexts of the changes that are taking place in the curriculum, its assessment and its control and so help them to decide their own priorities for action. Action needs to take a number of forms. Some will lead to the marrying of existing good practice to the forms of expression of the National Curriculum. Some will extend existing practice. Some will be to make sure that teachers' voices are heard about the desirability and practicability of what is proposed, and that they are heard by parents, the public at large, politicians and those charged with running the National Curriculum. We all need to recognize the changed position of teachers in this last respect. Formerly, teachers were, theoretically at least, responsible for what they taught. Criticisms from outside were usually met defensively. Now the National Curriculum is being decided nationally and teachers' stance can be positive, can relate requirements to resources and be concerned with the effects on the children of what others are deciding. It will be a great mistake to attempt to raise hackles about things that are mere Aunt Sallies or are trivial, for then the more serious arguments will be lost.

The book is not, in an academic sense, a history, though its purposes, as with the study of history, include the illumination of the present. Its intention is to look forward rather than to dwell on the past. What has already happened in this aspect of life as in others is of interest to most people mainly because it helps us to hazard what the future may hold.

The main period covered is from the publication of the Plowden Report[1] on primary education until the early 1990s. Earlier landmarks are mentioned if they add to the perspective. They include the 1944 Education Act for England and Wales, which established the right 'of all' to secondary education and so, almost by default, established primary education; and the report[2] of the Hadow Committee of 1931 which reaffirmed its use, in 1926, of the term 'primary' for the education of children up to 11, and also used the terms 'infant' for schools for children aged 5 to 7, and 'junior' for schools for children between 7 and 11.

Confusion continues to exist today because the Hadow Report used the term 'primary school' for a school taking children from 5 to 11 and also synonymously with 'junior school' but not with 'infant school'. In this book I shall use the term 'primary schools' to cover all schools where a majority of the children are somewhere between the ages of 3 and 11-plus. When wishing to refer to schools according to the specific age groups they cover, then I shall use the following terms:

Ages 5 to 11 Infant and Junior Schools
     5 to 12 First and Middle Schools
     5 to 7 Infant Schools
     5 to 8 5–8 First Schools
     5 to 9 5–9 First Schools
     7 to 11 Junior Schools
     8 to 12 8–12 Middle Schools
     9 to 13 9–13 Middle Schools

The terminology is made more difficult to interpret because some of the first five types of schools in the above list have nursery classes which take children from 3 years of age or, exceptionally, 2; others accept children at the *beginning of the school year* — 1st September to the following 31st August — in which they will be five; or at the *beginning of the term in which they will become 5*; or they are restricted to the Statutory Age by which Local Authorities must provide places, namely *the beginning of the term following a child's fifth birthday*.

Infant Schools generally pass children on to Junior Schools at the beginning of the school year in which the children will become 8, i.e. most are still 7. The exceptions, already 8, have birthdays in the first few days of September preceding the first day of the autumn term. Children transfer from 5 to 8 First Schools one year later, and from 5 to 9 First Schools two years later.

All but a handful of 9 to 13 Middle Schools are deemed to be secondary schools; all of the few examples of 9–14 or 10–14 middle schools are counted as secondary schools.

Combined Infant and Junior Schools or combined First and Middle Schools are provided usually because separate schools would be small, but sometimes as a matter of preference, when the combined school can have 500 or more pupils.

The establishment of First and Middle Schools was made possible by the Education Act of 1964, when Sir Edward (later Lord) Boyle was Secretary of State for Education. Pressure for changing the age of transfer from primary to secondary education came from a number of quarters. Some in secondary schools thought that the age range 11 to 19 was too wide and made it difficult to treat the 19-year-olds in ways that respected their maturity. Others, and they were probably the more influential, wanted to change to comprehensive secondary schooling and saw a re-jigging of the stages of schooling as a way of making the change from a selective system largely within the buildings available. Leicestershire under its Director of Education, Stuart Mason, had earlier split secondary schooling between 11–14 and 14–18 schools for much the same reasons; the West Riding of Yorkshire, under Alec (later Sir Alec) Clegg was known to favour the idea of Middle Schools and was among the first to adopt a 9–13 middle school system, with comprehensive upper schools, in some areas.

Notes

1. DES (1967) *Children and their Primary Schools, A report of Central Advisory Council for Education (England)*, (Plowden Report), Chairman Lady B. Plowden, London, HMSO (2 vols).
2. Board of Education (1931) *Report of the Consultative Committee on The Primary School*, (Hadow Report) Chairman Sir W. H. Hadow, CBE, London, HMSO.

Chapter 1

Children: Separately and Together

A neutral though slightly alarming statement about the purpose of schooling — an important part of the educational process — is that it exists to change children from what they otherwise might have been. If it is to have no effect, why spend the effort and money imposing school upon them? In both totalitarian and democratic societies, children are taught to become literate. In the former there might be emphasis on developing obedience and in the latter on individual responsibility. Wherever we are, the statement obliges us, when thinking about schooling, to think also about the children, about what they are like and how they change. That is why the first chapter of this book, mainly about the curriculum and its operation, is about them.

Of course, we have no difficulty in distinguishing between people, including children, and all other living things. Nevertheless, unless a school is on a remote island with only one pupil, each class will be made up of children of mixed age, mixed ability and mixed personality, no matter how much the headteacher may try to group like children together. Before we can consider to what extent schools should or can respond differently to different children we must recall some differences that are educationally significant.

One of the strongest and longest running trends in English education has been the growing concern for children as individuals. Both the Hadow and Plowden Reports placed great emphasis on the importance of taking children's natures into account when deciding how best to educate them. Both drew attention to differences between children of the same age, as have writers of other Reports since. The Hadow Report asserts[1] that:

at the age of five, children are spread out between the mental ages of about three and seven or eight, a total of four to five years. By the age of ten this range has doubled and it probably continues to enlarge till the end of puberty.

The Plowden Report pays early attention to children's growth and development on the grounds that:

At the heart of the educational process lies the child.[2]

Physical Growth

Plowden drew attention to differences in the rates of development of different parts of the body. The head and brain grow most during the first few years, so that the latter reaches about 90 per cent of its adult weight by the time a child is 5. Children grow taller more rapidly in the first months after birth than they will at any time later, even when they shoot up during puberty. Physical differences between groups and between individuals are also recounted. On average, boys are larger at birth, but girls catch up by six and go through their pubertal height spurt earlier than boys. Boys, when their turn comes, grow more rapidly than the girls did and experience a greater increase in muscular strength. Just as the Hadow Report spoke of mental age and skeletal growth, so the Plowden Report referred to skeletal or 'bone' age. The bones in the hand and wrist undergo a sequence of changes as people get older, and these can be plotted in series of X-rays. On this skeletal ladder, girls are some weeks more mature than boys at birth and up to two years ahead by puberty.

These statements about average ages by which children, or groups of children, reach certain levels of growth should, as with 'mental age' be treated cautiously:

Among boys of the same chronological age there is a wide range of bone age which, for eight year olds, stretches from six to ten 'years'.[3]

Plainly, the range for 8-year-old boys and girls together is wider than four 'years', and some girls are less mature in their bone structure than some boys of the same age. It is also important to remember that the rate of maturation is not constant from generation to generation. The Report drew attention to the secular trend in the lowering age of the onset of menstruation in a number of Western countries over a substantial period of time and an increase in the average height of children measured at the same ages.

Differences of achievement

Differences in Reading, Writing and Speaking

The interest in differences between children was picked up again in the Bullock Report of 1975, which followed an enquiry into the teaching of the English language. It quoted a witness as saying:

> . . . in a first-year secondary school class containing the full range of ability, the English teacher may encounter an extraordinarily wide spread in reading age (e.g., from seven to fourteen), and an accompanying wide divergence in maturity of reading interest and taste.[4]

That broad statement hides a maze of complexities. National surveys conducted by the National Foundation for Educational Research (NFER) for the Assessment of Performance Unit[5] (APU) have shown[6] that some children misinterpret what they read because they are not familiar with the concepts discussed and vocabulary used. They or others may have difficulty in locating the information they need to answer a question. In some cases, the more complex aspects of English grammar may cause a lack of understanding, though the grammatical system is not a hindrance to the majority. Stylistic variations cause difficulties for many, and the preconceptions children bring can put them off track. The 1982 report shows that very few 11-year-olds 'appeared to have trouble decoding the printed word.'[7]

The NFER design tests for use with children of a single year group and do not use the concept of, for example, 'reading age'. They provide tables that make it possible to convert raw scores directly to standardized scores. Whether it is reasonable to define a 'writing age' is questionable even within the kinds of uncertainties used in making judgements about mental ages, but no-one looking through the written work of children born in the same school year can fail to recognize that there are differences in the range and complexity of ideas expressed, the clarity of the description or message, adherence to 'standard' forms of English including syntax and spelling, the ability to catch and hold the reader's attention. The differences are in part consistent, in the sense that, for example, one child will again and again use a wider vocabulary than another; but inconsistent in the sense that children will swap order according to the accident of the subject of the writing and the states of their interests in it at the time. Work carried out for the APU indicates that about 3 per cent of 11-year-olds[8] (not in special schools) are in great difficulty with writing. Boys are more likely than girls to have negative attitudes towards writing and girls are more likely to be assessed as better able to express themselves in writing.

Children's writing is influenced by the ways in which they speak and they need to be made more aware of the differences between writing and speaking. Most 11-year-olds[9] can, to some degree, modify their speaking and listening to suit the circumstances; at the least, they may use different vocabularies, accents and grammar when in the playground as compared with those used in the classroom. Girls and boys are about equal in oral ability. Pupils' performance varies with the purpose of the communication. Individual pupils' spoken language may be either more or less advanced than their performance in reading and writing.

Differences in Mathematical Achievement

A reference to the differences between children in mathematics was made in the Cockroft Report,[10] which produced evidence to show a 'seven year' difference in achieving an understanding of place value.

When asked to write down the number that is 1 more than 6399, average children of 11 entered the correct number but average children of 10 did not. Additionally, some children of 7 carried out the task correctly and some of 14 did not. That is more evidence, it is said, of a 'seven year' range of ability towards the end of the primary school stage.

Surveys by the NFER for the APU reveal still more about mathematical differences between children. The *Primary Survey Report No. 2*,[11] included an account of 11-year-old children's attitudes to mathematics as shown in their responses to a questionnaire. The questions probed whether children liked mathematics, what they thought about the difficulty of the subject, and how far they believed it to be useful to learn. The mean scores in all three groups of questions were similar for boys and girls. When reflecting, more particularly, on their own competence rather than on the inherent difficulty of the subject, girls were more inclined than boys to suppose that they often got into difficulties and were surprised when they succeeded.

The Report quotes other examples of similar findings. Fewer girls than boys liked the more practical topics or found them easy. The (11-year-old) boys, on average, did better than the girls to a statistically significant degree[12] in five of the thirteen sub-categories of the written tests. The five are asterisked in the following full list: lines angles and shapes; symmetry, transformations and co-ordinates; money, time, weight and temperature*; length, area, volume and capacity*; concepts — whole numbers; concepts — decimals and fractions*; computation — whole numbers and decimals; computation — fractions; applications of number*; rate and ratio*; generalized arithmetic; sets and relations; probability and data representation. On average, children in schools in metropolitan areas scored significantly less well than children in non-metropolitan areas in nine of the sub-categories. In every sub-category, the mean score was substantially better for children in schools with fewer than 16 per cent on free school meals as compared with those in schools with 36 per cent or more on free school meals. Children in schools with less generous pupil: teacher ratios did better on average than children in other schools. Children in schools where there were fewer pupils in the 10-plus age group (i.e. smaller schools), on average, did better than children in schools with middling to large 10-plus age groups.

Scientific Achievement

The APU's *Science Report for Teachers: 1*[13] draws attention to other differences between children. For example, most 11-year-olds read the scales of simple measuring instruments correctly, but only a few took the step of repeating measurements or observations to check results. Most of the children classified objects on the basis of observed properties; about a half made predictions based on observations and used given information to make reasonable predictions; but only a few recorded the observation of fine details, observed the correct sequence of events or gave good explanations of how they arrvied at predictions. The Report records that at this age, the differences between boys and girls are not marked or consistent. Girls, on average, were slightly ahead in using graphs, tables and charts, in observing similarities and differences and in writing up descriptions of events. Boys, on average, were ahead in using measuring instruments, applying physical science concepts to problems and in recording quantitative results.

Differences of Personality and Behaviour

There are other differences between children. Some reference has already been made to self-perception. Most parents who have had more than one child will be aware of the differences of temperament that can be found in two who have drawn from the same genetic bank. They are more or less assertive, more or less confident, more or less sensitive to changes of circumstance, more or less given to flights of the imagination. They differ in what they notice and in what they care about. One may be balanced, precise and rhythmic when moving and the other clumsy and rough and erratic whether in walking and running, using a pencil or pen, or a shaping tool — descriptions that will almost invariably be too crude for two real children.

The Causes of Differences

One of the dangers of comparative lists of the kind just discussed is that someone might suppose that the differences revealed are examples of cause and effect. The most that can be said with certainty is that they are associations: other common but unrevealed factors may be responsible for the difference.

The differences are the result of two distinguishable but interrelated causes: the genetic make-up of the individual and the circumstances and experiences to which the individual has been subject.

Genetic Factors

By the time of the Plowden Report, opinion had moved further from the notion that the genetic inheritance was so powerful as virtually to fix an individual's capacities. The Report[14] concluded that:

the notion of the constancy of the I.Q. is biologically self-exploding as well as educationally explosive.

It pointed out that children's Intelligence Quotients (IQs) changed between 9 and 19 years of age to such an extent that 20 per cent changed either from being in the lower half to being in the upper half of scores or vice versa.

We need to remember that an IQ is not intelligence. It is the result of doing sums based on the scores a person achieves in answering questions or carrying out actions. In well-regarded intelligence tests there are many different sorts of questions. The Plowden Report refers to the Wechsler Intelligence Scale for Children (W.I.S.C.). That comprises 12 sections: information, comprehension, arithmetic, similarities, vocabulary, digit span, picture completion, picture arrangement, block design, object assembly, coding and mazes. Even so, aspects of thinking are left out. There is nothing, for example, on the ability to interpret the tone of voice or physical mannerisms when deducing what an oral message means. The pre-

7

sumptions are, first, that the areas chosen are sufficient to represent the ways in which intelligence manifests itself; and, second, that underneath the variety of thinking we do there is a single competence that can be called general intelligence. The general factor is expressed through and limits ability in aspects of behaviour, e.g. arithmetical ability, which might be further limited by environmental experience.

My personal observation of children and adults leads me to be agnostic in this matter to the point of being a borderline disbeliever. I am sure that the concept of a general factor of intelligence is not a helpful one in primary education, partly because every child and adult I have met, except for one young adult who was blind, deaf and unable to sit up or crawl, has been capable of learning more — any inherent limit of learning has not manifested itself — and especially so because acceptance of the concept inclines people to believe that it is possible to judge what a child may be capable of doing, or more usually not doing, in the medium or long term.

Environmental Factors

Social Class

The Plowden Council built upon earlier views about the effects of the environment on children's performance in school. The Hadow Report[15] expressed the view that:

> In the past eugenic and biometric investigators have rightly emphasised the effects of heredity; but there is now (1931) an increasing tendency to believe that they have underestimated the effects of the environment.

The Plowden Report took the thought to the point of recommending the indentification of deprived areas where the children had special educational needs.[16] These were to be called Educational Priority Areas (EPAs) and be subject to 'positive descrimination' in the distribution of funds and as a consequence, resources, particularly teachers and nursery education. The criteria that might be used in identification were: the proportion of unskilled and semi-skilled manual workers; the presence of large families; the numbers in receipt of State benefits, including free school meals (the unemployed were not mentioned specifically in 1967); overcrowding and sharing of houses; poor attendance and truancy; proportions of retarded, disturbed or handicapped children; incomplete families (what we would now call single-parent families); and the number of children unable to speak English. It pointed out that no formula is perfect and that some special groups like canal-boat children and gypsies (again the terminology has altered and we would now talk about Travellers' children) also have special needs.

The recommendation has certainly had consequences. A. H. Halsey was commissioned by the Department of Education and Science (DES) to conduct a major research project which concluded that:[17]

1. It is possible to define a unit through which to apply the principle of positive discrimination;
2. Standards in educational priority areas can be raised economically by providing pre-school opportunities;
3. The development of community schools has 'powerful implications for community regeneration';
4. Partnership between families and schools in EPAs can be improved;
5. The quality of teaching can be improved in EPA schools;
6. Action-research (which this was) is an effective method of policy formation and practical innovation;
7. The EPA can be no more than a part, though an important one, of a comprehensive social movement towards community development and community redevelopment in a modern industrial society.

For a time, teachers in identified schools were paid an additional allowance. The results were disappointing, for the effect was, if anything, to persuade teachers already in the schools to stay in them without giving them an incentive to change their teaching practices.

Many Local Education Authorities distributed funds and teachers so that schools in areas of relative poverty had better than average provision. The Inner London Education Authority (ILEA) devised a scheme[18] for funding schools differentially, entitled *The Alternative Use of Resources scheme*. This gave schools more freedom of choice in what to purchase, including human resources, than they had with their basic funds. Account was taken of most of the criteria suggested in the Plowden Report, omitting — in the 1983 version — housing conditions and, intriguingly, the numbers of children who were handicapped or falling behind in their performance, but adding ethnic family background and pupil mobility. It is certainly odd at first sight that the one direct measure of pupils' performance in school was left out of the list. One argument was that extra money should not be given to schools that are themselves inefficient and so cause children to achieve poorly. I understand the dilemma, but take the view that the children should be given priority and that action needs to be taken in the children's interests. That may well cost more, though the action chosen and funded should be closely overseen by the Local Education Authority (LEA). Just supplying more of what schools already have is not likely to improve children's achievements. There is also a need to focus the extra provision and effort and even to modify practice — for example to take care to increase children's confidence in their own dialect while at the same time teaching them to use forms of language that are more widely used in education, commerce and business generally.

Nursery provision

The Central Government's Urban Programme, which began in 1969, approved the establishment of some 20,000 new places in nursery schools and classes as well as day nurseries, community centres and classes in English as a second language. The 1972 White Paper, *Education: A Framework for Expansion*,[19] adopted when Margaret Thatcher was Secretary of State for Education, included substantial proposals for an expansion of nursery education with the aim of meeting the Plowden Council's recommendation of providing for 90 per cent of 4-year-olds and 50 per cent of 3-year-olds within ten years. The sudden changes in oil costs and supply in 1973/4 severely truncated that aim. The Government had intended that priority would 'be given in the early stages of the programme to areas of disadvantage',[20] and the bulk of what was provided went to such areas.

It has to be said that it is hard to get conclusive evidence that what is provided before age 5 has a long term educational benefit for a child — which is not at all to deny the importance of nursery education. This makes it hard to know how a teacher's expectations should change with the knowledge that a child has or has not had nursery education. There is often quoted evidence that summer-born children, on average, do less well than autumn-born children, and throughout school life, but it is very difficult to know whether, or how far, that is because the former are the youngest in their year group and how far it may be because they have had less schooling.

Cultural and religious differences

The Plowden Report and the ILEA Alternative Use of Resources Scheme both took notice of the fact that society in England has become more diverse since the 1940s, with many ethnic groups, cultures and religions being represented. By 1985, it was possible to report[21] that children attending ILEA schools spoke, between them, 147 different languages. The figure is now more than 150.

The 50 schools studied in the *ILEA Junior School Project* were reported[22] as being a reflection of the ethnic composition of Inner London as a whole. In these schools, the largest percentages of pupils from ethnic minority backgrounds were from families with Caribbean backgrounds (nearly 13 per cent) and Asian backgrounds (7 per cent). Pupils from black and other ethnic minority groups made up 40 per cent of the schools' pupils. In the sample, nearly 16 per cent of the children did not use English as their first language; 34 other languages were identified as being used, of which Greek was the most common, followed by Bengali/Sylheti, Urdu, Turkish and Gujerati. Of course, there are some schools in England with no experience of children from families with overseas backgrounds — at least in living memory. But one may meet, for example, children of Polish extraction in rural parts of Lincolnshire, of Italian extraction in parts of Bedfordshire, and of Chinese extraction in small towns throughout England. No children, anywhere, should be denied the advantage of learning about the culturally and religiously diverse community of the country in which they live. The task may be all the more difficult in schools that are themselves uni-cultural.

The Rampton and Swann Reports

The Rampton and Swann Reports[23] were commissioned by the Central Government to consider the educational implications of these changes in society. The writers of the first were disturbed by the relatively low school achievement, on average, of children with Caribbean family backgrounds as compared with children from white indigenous families and from some Asian backgrounds. Their worries are shared by the children's parents. The Swann Report confirms the earlier worries but suggests that the differences of performance between racial groups are diminishing. It urged that all schools should make children aware that they live in a multi-racial society and help them to understand and accept the implications. Some recent work, notably the ILEA Junior School Project referred to earlier, has suggested that the picture may actually be more complex than was supposed. Children from some Asian groups may — the figures on which the assessments are based are small — do only about as well as those from Caribbean backgrounds. Children from families of Turkish and Greek origins may also, on average, make less than ordinary progress. The researchers have attempted to eliminate the effects of other factors such as social class and sex, which also affect average scores.

The reasons for the differences are not easy to be sure about and to counter. The Rampton Report spoke of 'unintentional' racism as a contributory factor since it led to white teachers having unduly low expectations of the children, and to low expectations of career prospects by the children. Some teachers were said to be prejudiced against the Caribbean form of English usage. There was also thought to be too little support for the schools from Caribbean families.

It is important to remember that one of the Rampton Report's findings was that stereotyping is disadvantageous. This Chapter, and particularly these few paragraphs, could inadvertently reinforce stereotyping. There is a considerable difficulty in discussing any of the differences between groups of children, whether chosen according to social class, sex, race or any other criterion. Some of the differences should be thought about and action taken by teachers to minimize disadvantages and to spread advantages more widely. But no individual child should be thought to carry a disadvantage simply because he or she is a member of a particular class, sex or race. In my view we are not helped by graphs showing only the average scores for groups of children. All graphs should show both the average scores and, spreading out from the averages, the range of scores achieved by the sub-groups of children so that the overlaps between one group and others are clear. This is a practice used to good effect in the NFER reports for the APU.

Children with special educational needs

Since before the Warnock Report[24] — even the best reports have the knack of sharpening up what is already happening rather than starting much that is new — ordinary schools (now referred to as 'mainstream' schools) have been increasingly inclined to admit children with learning difficulties arising from physical, sensory, mental and behavioural causes. The trend has strengthened since the Report and since the 1981 Education Act. Teachers in mainstream schools are now more likely than they were to be teaching children with moderate learning difficulties. They may also have children, or at least one child, in the class with a disability that would previously have been regarded as requiring the child to be placed in a special school, for example a child with spina bifida, or severe hearing impairment, or poor sight.[25]

Age and maturity

Quite apart from the differences between children of the same age, there are differences within a person as he or she ages. Some have already been referred to, for example skeletal maturity and those arising from differences of experience. The Hadow Reports and the Plowden Report were strongly influenced by the views of Jean Piaget, who, formerly a zoologist, began observing children as a psychologist in Geneva in the early 1920s. The essentials of his perceptions were reinforced, though sometimes with new terminology, by people like Jerome Bruner working in the USA. Like many others, they take the view that learners assimilate new ideas and skills, attaching new knowledge to old, and also may modify — accommodate — what they supposed they knew in the light of new experiences. Both Piaget and Bruner also took the view that children pass through distinguishable stages in their intellectual development. Piaget postulated four phases. In the *sensori-motor phase*, a child was said to move from what seem to be un-coordinated reflex responses to more complex patterns of activity, and begin to accept that inanimate and animate objects persist. The period of *intutitive thought* was regarded as a transitional stage when children took notice of only one relationship at a time, actions were not thought of as being reversible and judgements were frequently intuitive and based on perception. The period of *concrete operations* was thought to cover most of the primary school stage during which children came to notice stable and reversible relationships in concrete (not necessarily practical but certainly specific) situations. In the fourth stage of *formal operations* children were said to become capable of logical thought, using symbolic and abstract material. Essentially, as a colleague of Piaget's put it,[26] these stages indicate that 'the child mind so often appears opaque to adult observation . . . because it belongs to *a different kind* of thought — autistic or symbolic thought . . .'

Piaget worked and was an influence during a period when children were dressed differently from adults. As they and adults have come to be dressed more and more alike — I do no more than observe the juxtaposition — so Piaget's ideas have come under more and more critical examination. Margaret Donaldson[27] among others has drawn attention to the problem of interpreting what children do and say, and to the importance of the context in which they are asked to respond. One of the great benefits of Piaget's work was that it led teachers to think much harder about what children said and did. The disadvantage was that his ideas seemed to some to offer little hope of accelerating progress, though he never supposed that the stages were of fixed duration from child to child.

There is a more optimistic view now, that teaching can make a difference. I have to say that my observation of children and teachers leads me to believe that optimism is justified. Research evidence on very young babies suggests that they do continue to look for something that has been hidden behind a screen, i.e. to suppose that it persists.[28] Such sensitive periods for learning as there are, for example in learning to talk, do not appear to inhibit the ordinary conduct of schooling, and it would be very surprising if the gradual introduction of formal education had not, almost instinctively, led to a reasonable conformity between its purposes and the timing of its conduct. David Ausubel[29] would argue that the need is to introduce children to new experiences that they may think about in the light of what they already know, so adding to or adjusting existing knowledge and, through postulation and discussion, formulate higher-level ideas. What looked like a different form of thinking by young children may be the result of their having to hypothesize from too little experience, or too limited a range of experience. I have no doubt personally that discussion is as important as the direct experience. It needs to be handled with great sensitivity and not be taken to the point where children are mouthing the teacher's words.

Summary

A class or teaching group is made up of individual children who differ from one another in a variety of ways that affect them educationally. The differences are such that it is dangerous to suppose that two children who are similar in one regard will be similar in another. That is true whether considering two children of the same age, the same sex, the same social class or the same race; or whether considering two children from different sub-groups. A child who reads well may not necessarily write legibly or spell well. He or she may be quick to grasp the differences and the relationship between perimeter, area and volume, yet stumble in arithmetic.

Putting children in order according to one criterion is *at best* only an approximate and general guide to their order according to another criterion, and not just in obviously different things like designing scientific experiments and painting pictures, but also in apparently connected things such as speaking and writing. What is more, even on the one criterion, the order today is unlikely to be just the same as the order last month.

Furthermore, it has to be remembered, the experiences of many of today's children are different in some important respects from those of their parents and their teachers when children. They are more likely to be familiar with the ways in which electronic devices work. They may well have access to a video-recorder as well as to a television set, and although many watch some programmes that some adults would prefer they did not, they also watch others designed for them, nature programmes designed for all, and catch at least snatches of current affairs and news programmes. Many have a micro-computer, and even though it may be used predominantly for games, the games may include 'board' games or tests of logic and association as well as those testing the speed of physical reaction. In most classes there is probably at least one child more familiar with the technological hardware than is his or her teacher. Only the rashest of forecasters would suppose that the rate of change will slow down significantly.

Faced with such complexity and flux what are teachers to do and what can society reasonably expect?

The chapters that follow flow from that question, but I believe that is already plain that teachers cannot possibly treat each child wholly individually and that it would not be in a child's best interests to do so. One important advantage of attending school is that children can learn to live and work within a variety of groups and with children who are different from themselves. Nor is it educationally sensible to treat all of the children in a class as though they were identical. It is equally plain that children cannot be arranged in homogenous groups for two, three, four different aspects of their learning and even when grouped for a single purpose will not remain the same for a term or a year. The implications for the organization of teaching, of children and their learning are considerable.

The implications are also of great importance when deciding on curricular priorities for all children and for individuals. How far and in what respects should teachers consciously be striving to make children more alike? Make no mistake, much of what a school does is for that purpose, and we can only keep the process under control if we face the question. I do want schools to reduce the gaps between children's achievements in English and in mathematics, for example, and to do so by increasing the achievements of those who manage less well without detriment to those who do well. I certainly agree with those who think that schools can make a difference in this respect. Of course it is necessary to raise one's expectations of children from some groups. This is sometimes made more difficult by the ways that information about sub-groups of children is presented. Though it is true, to judge from the evidence, that children from metropolitan areas do less well in mathematics than do children from non-metropolitan areas, we must keep reminding ourselves that quite a lot of children from the first do better than quite a lot of children from the second. When ethnic groups are compared we have to remind ourselves even more firmly that averages are likely to be misleading when applied to individuals.

It is, on the whole, easier to recognize and respond to substantial differences than to modest differences. Teachers everywhere have much to learn from the successful teaching of English to children who come to school with little or no English. The schools adapt themselves not only to the children but also to their parents. They make sure that parents and children know that the home language is respected. Where indigenous children come speaking a non-school form of English, attitudes are often, sadly, different: the home language is regarded as inferior and that message is conveyed to children and parents. For children who speak another language at home, the object is, and is understood to be, to add standard English to the children's competencies, not to replace the home language. So it should be in the case of children speaking Cockney, Scouse or Caribbean dialects.

But if some aspects of schooling are directed towards making children more alike, others should stimulate differences. Most problems can be solved in more than one way. Present capacity, personality, the availability of tools and equipment, an accident of the moment, each may determine the preferred route to a solution. The noticing and discussion of differences of approach help children to develop insight into their own ways of working and contribute to one of the most fundamental purposes of education: to know one's self. The solutions may differ in relatively trivial ways, such as the orders in which calculations are worked through; they may also differ fundamentally in that one child copes with his or her feelings most effectively through dance or painting, another through words, and yet another through sublimation.

For teachers in action there can be no blueprint which determines how a child or a class must be treated. As we shall see, however, that is not to say that there are no permissible guidelines either in what is to be taught or in the pedagogy that enables teaching and learning to occur.

Notes

1. Board of Education (1931) *Report of the Consultative Committee on the Primary School*, (Hadow Report) Chairman Sir W. H. Hadow, CBE, paragraph 35, London, HMSO.
2. DES (1967) *Children and their Primary Schools*, (Plowden Report), Vol. 1, paragraph 9 ff., London, HMSO.
3. DES (1967) Plowden Report, *op. cit.*, Vol. 1, paragraph 14.
4. DES (1975) *A language for life*, (Bullock Report), Committee of Inquiry, Chairman, Sir Alan Bullock, London, HMSO.
5. The establishment of the Assessment of Performance Unit (APU) was announced by the Department of Education and Science in 1974. It has worked mainly by commissioning NFER and University Departments to undertake, for example, studies of children's abilities in English, a foreign language, mathematics, science, technology. Its reports, including summary reports, have been published by the DES, the Department of Education Northern Ireland and the Welsh Office. It is now attached to the School Examinations and Assessment Council. See also Chapter 5 for its terms of reference.
6. Gorman, T. (1986) *The Framework for the Assessment of Language*, DES/APU Windsor, NFER-Nelson.
7. DES/APU (1982) *Language Performance in Schools: Primary Survey Report No. 2*, London, HMSO.

8. White, J. (1986) *The Assessment of Writing*, pp. 8–9, Windsor, APU/NFER-Nelson.
9. Maclure, M. and Hargreaves, M. (1986) *Speaking and Listening, Assessment at Age 11*, p. 4 ff., Windsor, APU/NFER-Nelson.
10. DES (1982) *Mathematics Counts*, (Cockcroft Report) Committee of Inquiry chaired by Dr W. H. Cockcroft, paragraphs 342 and 436, London, HMSO.
11. DES/APU (1981) *Mathematical Development, Primary Survey Report No. 2*, pp. 40 ff., London, HMSO.
12. *ibid.*, paragraph 4.31.
13. DES/APU (1983) *Science Report for Teachers: 1, Science at Age 11*, London, DES.
14. DES (1967) Plowden Report, *op. cit.*, paragraphs 60 ff.
15. Board of Education (1931) Hadow Report, *op. cit.*, paragraph 48.
16. DES (1967) Plowden Report, *op. cit.*, paragraphs 153ff.
17. Halsey, A. (Ed.) (1972) *Educational Priority, Volume 1: E.P.A. Problems and Policies* pp. 180ff., London, HMSO.
18. ILEA (1985) *Improving Primary Schools, Report of Committee on Primary Education*, chaired by Norman Thomas, London, ILEA.
19. DES (1972) Cmnd. 5174 *Education: A Framework for Expansion* London, HMSO.
20. *ibid.*, paragraph 28.
21. ILEA (1985) *Improving Primary Schools, op. cit.*, paragraph 1.28.
22. Mortimore, P., Sammons, P., Stoll, L., Lewis, D. and Ecob, R. (1988) *School Matters, The Junior Years*, p. 92, Wells, Open Book Publishers.
23. DES (1981) Cmnd. 8273 *West Indian Children in Our Schools*, Interim Report of the Committee of Inquiry into the Education of Children from Minority Ethnic Groups, Chairman M. A. Rampton, London, HMSO,
   DES (1985) Cmnd. 9453 *Education for All*, Final Report of the Committee of Inquiry into the Education of Children from Minority Ethnic Groups, Chairman Lord Swann, London, HMSO.
24. DES (1978) Cmnd. 7212 *Special Educational Needs, Report of the Committee of Inquiry into the Education of Handicapped Children and Young People*, Chairman H. M. Warnock, London, HMSO.
25. See also page 124.
26. Claparède, E. (1960) in preface to Piaget, J., *The Language and Thought of the Child*, London, Routledge and Kegan Paul.
27. Donaldson, M., (1978) *Children's Minds*, London, Fontana.
28. Brierley, J. (1978) *Growing and Learning*, London, Ward Lock Educational.
29. Ausubel, D. P., Novak, J. D. and Hanesian, H. (1978) *Educational Psychology: A Cognitive View*, New York, Holt, Rinehart and Winston.

Chapter 2

What Shall Children be Taught?

One of the difficulties in writing about primary education, and probably other aspects of life as well, is that the words have to proceed in single file, folded up into lines though they are for the convenience of reading. What children are like, what schools intend to teach them and what they learn (the last two would ideally be the same but sometimes are not), and what we provide to enable the learning and teaching to take place are interdependent aspects of the educational process; each affects and is affected by the others. It sometimes seems that it would be possible to get nearer to reality if accounts could be written in at least four lines simultaneously, as music may be. What follows in this Chapter pays attention to what children are or should be taught in general rather than particular terms and it is important while reading to keep in mind the effects of the natures of the children, the form and volume of resourcing and the shifting circumstances in which the education service operates.

Process: Content: Objectives

A number of assumptions lie behind the previous paragraph. One relates to a notion of child-centredness that has beeen constructed upon if not wholly drawn from the Hadow and Plowden Reports. It has been well expressed by A. V. Kelly,[1] who argues for an empirical approach to the curriculum in which the processes of learning are what matter. The notion is questioned that there is a fixed body of knowledge, encapsulated in curricular subjects, which must be transmitted. To adopt such an idea in determining the curriculum is said to deny what is known of the ways children develop and learn and leads to educating children through the pursuit of objectives, often behavioural, that are external to primary education; such an approach also leads to schools being judged by criteria that are external to them.

I have sympathy with the idealism of that point of view. I do not hold to it as a sufficient guide to the curriculum because I believe that the dangers to which it gives rise are as great, perhaps even greater, than the dangers it warns against. The education of an individual occurs at the meeting place of that person and his or her circumstances. For our present purposes, that place is school. The shape of the building, the materials, books and people inside it — teachers, ancillary workers and especially other children — condition the pupil's learning. What the teachers do and say, how they respond to what the pupils do and say, all influence not only how the pupils learn but also what they learn. Anyone who doubts that is so should read Stephen Rowland's[2] and Michael Armstrong's[3] accounts of their work in primary school classrooms from the point of view of what the children did and became interested in and why. It was Rowland, not the children, who chose the Fibonacci number series. I do not imply any criticism. He, like all teachers and like all schools, acted as a sieve, allowing some learning material through and rejecting other. The danger of an over-concentration on the process model of the curriculum is that the sieve will be mindless.

The pursuit of objectives can also lead to trouble. They are difficult to define except in terms of what children do. Too much precision either leads to having so many objectives that in practice no one can take account of them all, or each is pursued laboriously in turn and there is no sense of the whole, rather like trying to count a million in a number system that has no arrangement for grouping numbers or place value. Even remembering the number names would require a vocabulary greater than anyone now has. If objectives are too broad then it is difficult to get agreement on whether they have been reached: children of x years should know the main countries of the world and their capitals. Presumably China should be in, but must it be Beijing or will Peking do? Should South Africa be included? It's certainly in the news if that is what is meant by 'main'. Saudi Arabia? Quatar? Argentina? Uruguay? There are more difficult examples than countries and capitals.

Yet, any teacher with a class is likely to have in mind some idea or skill or set of facts that at least one child should be better at by the end of a day, or a week, or longer. It will be a minor triumph if Gary can acquire the habit of writing a 'd' in such a way that others will not mistake it for a 'b'. By the end of this week, Della will be quite familiar with the idea that the second digit from the right represents 20 and not 2. By the end of term, all of the children are going to know how the books are arranged in the school library, and where to find those they require without having to seek help. It would be as wrong to dismiss the usefulness of objectives in teaching as it would be to lose sight of the importance of the processes by which children's education proceeds. Objectives are generally more useful aids to direction in the short term than in the long term.

Aims: Directions of Travel

Quite a lot of the discussion about primary education and where it is taking the children has been about aims rather than objectives. There is no final objective to the school's task in teaching children to read and write, or to grow in social competence, or to play and appreciate music. In this sense, what children should be taught depends on what they already know. Regard has to be paid also to what they do not know and would, in the broadest sense, find useful either immediately or later — though not with such a gap in time that the memory has by then failed or become scarred and twisted beyond use. What they will find useful depends upon what they go on to do and think about, much of which is influenced and even determined by events outside their control and, much of it, outside a school's control.

Some of the difficulties in getting down to practicalities are immediately obvious. How do you discover what children know? That is much more difficult than people sometimes suppose, and will be discussed later, when considering assessment.

What do children *need to learn how to do*? At one level that seems simple enough. They need to improve their abilities to communicate: through speaking and listening, reading and writing, through diagrams, pictures, graphs and numbers, through movement and music, through the use of machines — mechanical and electronic — and the use of tools and instruments. Communication is probably as often with oneself as with others. They need to learn better how to work and play in a group and also to operate alone. They need to extend their capacities to organize and shape materials and to tend plants; and to respect and relate to animal life. Some of the means of communication and ways of shaping materials, relationships and events are constant or change only slowly from one generation to the next but others, for example electronic devices and power driven tools, have changed fast; who supposed when the Plowden Report was published that 3- and 4-year-olds could find a use for a microcomputer, use an infra-red switching device, or that there would be an electric saw that infants could use safely?

In brief, children need to learn to interpret the messages their senses are receiving and to take action and transmit their own feelings, ideas and wishes in ways that are likely to be effective. What do children *need to know about*? They need to know something of what others know and believe, and how people manage or formerly managed their lives, in circumstances that are similar to their own and in others that are dissimilar. They need to appreciate the effects on their lives of what other people do or have done, whether in the past or in the wider world today. They need to know about the characteristics of materials, plants and animals, of the ways they behave, and what opportunities and obligations arise for us.

As Lady Warnock most succinctly put it in her brief guide to the Warnock Report, the aims are:

> first, to increase a child's knowledge of the world he lives in and his imaginative understanding, both of the possibilities of that world and of his own responsibilities in it; and, secondly, to give him as much independence and self sufficiency as he is capable of, by teaching him those things he must know in order to find work and to manage and control his own life.[4]

Some Principles the Curriculum Should Exhibit

Sir Keith (now Lord) Joseph had some important things to say[5] about what the parts of the curriculum should provide between them. First, they should together make up a broad curriculum both in the development of personal qualities and in the range of knowledge and skills to which children are introduced. Second, what they contain should be relevant to the real world and to the pupil's experience of it. Third, there should be differentiation to allow for variations in the abilities and aptitudes of the pupils. Fourth, the various parts need to be balanced in such a way as to optimize the contribution that each can make to the total education of the pupil. Each of these principles is open to wide interpretation. I hope that *breadth* is taken to require concern for children's physical, mental, aesthetic, moral, spiritual and social development, for helping them to become better informed and able to use information, and for giving them opportunities to use their imaginations. *Relevance* to the real world should certainly be judged in relation to the children's current experiences but should also be concerned with extending experience; relevance should take account of life as a whole, the immediate and the longer term, of which earning a living is a part but not everything. It is plain common sense to take account of the *differences* between pupils but that should not lead to children being treated in isolation nor to an assumption that the range of differences found today should always occur. A more sophisticated view of *balance* is required than that often found, which assumes that balance can be settled by regular allocations of time on the timetable rather than by assessing what children know and can do: time is an artefact of balance, not vice versa.

The implications of that view of balance are significant. They are well illustrated by a 6-year-old who might have been called Tony, but wasn't. His teacher noticed that he much preferred to engage in activities that had clear-cut outcomes. If asked what five eighteens are his eyes lit up, he put a tongue momentarily in his cheek, and then said '90'. His teacher gave him a potted chrysanthemum and some coloured tissue papers and asked him to make a 'stained-glass' pattern on a classroom windowpane, imitating as nearly as possible the colours of the flowers. She thought he was good at manipulating numbers compared with most 6-year-olds, but the change of activity was not intended to be a reward. She had also noticed that he became anxious when dealing with circumstances in which there was no clear-cut answer and decided that he needed to come to terms with the notion of approximating. She might, of course, have chosen measurement to bring the point home. What is interesting is her conception of balance between different aspects of Tony's behaviour: what is sometimes called a profile of development. There was no suggestion that the different aspects of learning could be equated precisely, but she did seek some broad correlation: balance. She did not start by asking herself whether mathematics and art(?) had had their due amounts of time. She assessed what the child could do and arranged the learning times accordingly. It is easy to see why that would be difficult to do in a programme arranged around specialist teaching as is the usual case in a secondary school, but that is one of the deficiencies of fixed timetabling. Other systems, as we shall see, have their own deficiencies, especially if they are elevated to principles.

Some Official Statements on Curricular Aims

By the Government, Central and Local

Between 1977 and 1985, the DES produced a series of documents containing proposed general aims for education in schools[6] that seemed to gain broad acceptance. The differences are sufficiently slight to make it worth quoting only the final version:

1. to help pupils to develop lively, enquiring minds, the ability to question and argue rationally and to apply themselves to tasks, and physical skills;
2. to help pupils to acquire understanding, knowledge and skills relevant to adult life and employment in a fast-changing world;
3. to help pupils to use language and number effectively;

4. to help pupils to develop personal moral values, respect for religious values, and tolerance of other races, religions and ways of life;
5. to help pupils to understand the world in which they live, and the inter-dependence of individuals, groups and nations;
6. to help pupils appreciate human achievements and aspirations.

Although these aims did find general agreement, some thought that there were omissions. A number of LEAs produced their own statements on the curriculum, mainly as the result of prompting by the DES.[7] In its discussion document[8] produced in 1983, Northamptonshire Education Committee suggested that the schools should also be expected to 'help pupils to be creative' and that more emphasis should be placed 'on the way in which the curriculum should fulfil the child's needs today and tomorrow as well as those of adult life in a changing society.' Adult life is a remote concept for young children. These points were reiterated in the more general and substantive document[9] published in 1985, which also argued for a curriculum that is continuous for children from 3 to 18.

In *Better Schools*[10] the expectations of primary schools are that they should:

place substantial emphasis on achieving competence in the use of language (which in Wales may be Welsh as well as English; but which does not normally encompass foreign languages);

place substantial emphasis on achieving competence in mathematics, in accordance with the recommendations of the Cockcroft Report;

introduce pupils to science;

lay the foundation of understanding in religious education, history and geography, and the nature and values of British society;

introduce pupils to a range of activities in the arts;

provide opportunities throughout the curriculum for craft and practical work leading up to some experience of design and technology and of solving problems;

provide moral education, physical education and health education;

introduce pupils to the nature and use in school and in society of new technology;

give pupils some insight into the adult world, including how people earn their living.

If the word 'substantial' had been included in the reference to science then all that was to come in the National Curriculum, and more, was contained.

By the Schools Council

The Schools Council[11] was set up in 1964, just a year after the Plowden Council began its work. For the most part, it worked by financing projects, at first nationally and then more locally, on parts of the curriculum. Among the most influential of the large scale projects concerning primary education were Breakthrough to Literacy, Science 3–13 and Joan Tough's work on language development with young children[12] The first was one of the rare examples of a Schools Council primary schools' project including the development of materials for children to use: sets of cards with words that children can use in constructing their own reading material and books for them to read. The second relied, almost entirely, on written advice to teachers on how to develop science teaching and assess it, though there were related short courses. The third depended considerably on working groups of teachers trying out ideas and commenting upon their effectiveness.

It was some time before the Schools Council produced a general statement on the curriculum for primary schools except for a review of the *Aims of Primary Education*,[13] published in 1975, which was mainly concerned with reporting what teachers said their aims were.

The *Practical Curriculum*,[14] a more prescriptive document, was published in 1981 and followed by *Primary Practice*[15] in October, 1983, only weeks before the Council was finally closed down by the Secretary of State in January, 1984. The former identified six ways in which schools have the capacity to help their pupils:

1. to acquire knowledge, skills and practical abilities, and the will to use them;
2. to develop qualities of mind, body, spirit, feeling and imagination;
3. to appreciate human achievements in art, music, science, technology and literature;
4. to acquire understanding of the social, economic and political order, and have a reasoned set of attitudes, values and beliefs;
5. to prepare for their adult lives at home, at work, at leisure, and at large, as consumers and citizens;

and, it was said, most important of all:

6. to develop a sense of self-respect, the capacity to live as independent, self-motivating adults and the ability to function as contributing members of co-operative groups.

Age and ability should be respected, and each school, year group and class required more specific aims. For example, the list suggested for a primary school was:

1. to read fluently and accurately, with understanding, feeling and discrimination;
2. to develop a legible style of handwriting and satisfactory standards of spelling, syntax, punctuation and usage;
3. to communicate clearly and confidently in speech and writing, in ways appropriate for various occasions and purposes;
4. to listen attentively and with understanding;
5. to learn how to acquire information from various sources,

and to record information and findings in various ways;

6. to apply computational skills with speed and accuracy;
7. to understand the application of mathematical ideas in various situations in home, classroom, school and local area;
8. to observe living and inanimate things, and to recognize characteristics such as pattern and order;
9. to master basic scientific ideas;
10. to investigate solutions and interpret evidence, to analyze and to solve problems;
11. to develop awareness of self and sensitivity to others, acquire a set of moral values and the confidence to make and hold to moral judgements, and develop habits of self-discipline and acceptable behaviour;
12. to be aware of geographical, historical and social aspects of the local environment and the national heritage, and to be aware of other times and places;
13. to acquire sufficient control of self or of tools, equipment and instruments to be able to use music, drama and several forms of arts and crafts as means of expression;
14. to develop agility and physical co-ordination, confidence in and through physical activity, and the ability to express feeling through movement.

The Relation Between Consensus and Meaning

The public debate on education between the mid-1970s and mid-1980s was essentially directed towards establishing a consensus on what schools are for, and what their priorities should be. A difficulty about reaching a consensus is that it requires finding a level of generality that everyone, or at least the great majority, can accept. Few will doubt that we should aim to educate boys and girls to become good men and good women. We may have strongly different views about what goodness consists of. It is one thing to agree that children should master basic scientific ideas, but quite another to get agreement on the practical meanings of 'master' or 'basic', and even 'scientific ideas' may mean different things to different people.

Anyone wishing to pass an hour or two in harmless amusement could go through any of the lists quoted, deliberately producing what they would regard as unlikely but arguable examples of what the items could mean.

Nevertheless, it was helpful to have both central and local Government declaring themselves in favour of a broad curriculum, especially given the public discussion about whether primary schools should limit their interests to the teaching of reading, writing and arithmetic — something not even the late Victorian Codes required — or whether they should take on board post-Newtonian ideas in mathematics and recent, i.e. twentieth century, ideas in science. It was also helpful because of the differences of practice between schools that had little or nothing to do with differences between their children but derived from the differences of training and inclination of teachers. The curriculum does need to be multi-faceted and it does need to be in step with life outside schools.

The Curriculum in Action

In the first weeks of 1980, Her Majesty's Inspectorate (HMI) produced a short statement, *A View of the Curriculum*,[16] with general sections and a part devoted specifically to primary schools. This document, like the DES contributions to follow, drew to a considerable extent on what HMI had reported in their 1978 national survey of primary schools.[17] That report found that primary schools generally were giving high priority to the teaching of reading, writing, mathematics, physical education, art and music. Observational and experimental science was less than common; there was less work in crafts than was desirable, and geography and history, often taught through topics, tended to be repetitive, lacked progression and generally paid insufficient regard to the multi-cultural nature of our society. Religious education was part of the programme of schools, but there was too little attention to faiths other than Christianity. A broad curriculum was necessary to cover the range of teaching and learning in today's society and also because of the opportunity that breadth provided for using and extending skills of literacy and numeracy and a range of other skills, for example observing, measuring, using tools and instruments. Many children, especially among those most advanced in any class, would benefit if they were given more demanding work. Differences in the children and differences in local circumstances and facilities properly give rise to some curricular differences.

Taking England as a whole, primary schools covered the curricular range necessary. A foreign language was still being taught in some places where the provision and also the opportunities for development in secondary schools did not warrant the inclusion. There was, however, much more inconsistency from one school to another than was often supposed. It was possible to say that a number of activities took place in 80 per cent or more of the classes whose work was inspected. They included such things as:

Language: teaching children to follow instructions, hand-writing practice, writing narratives;

Mathematics: calculating with whole numbers, the estimation and measurement of length, weight, area, volume and time, learning to recognize relationships in geometrical shape;

Aesthetic and physical education: singing; two or three dimensional work showing evidence of pattern or colour or texture or form; 11-year-olds swam; 7-year-olds practised the skills of gymnastics, games or swimming;

Social abilities and moral education: work was done to promote reliability and responsible attitudes, and children worked and played as members of groups.

This extract is intended to do no more than give a flavour of the original list of 35 items, some of them multiple and most but not all applying to the classes for 7-, 9- and 11-year-olds in the survey.[18]

However, only a half of the classes included all of the '80 per cent' items in English; the fraction for mathematics was, interestingly, higher at two-thirds, and one wonders whether that was because of the domination of a few text books series in the subject. Only two-fifths of the classes at any age included all the items for mathematics and language together. When classes were counted only if they included all of the items, they totalled less than a third of classes for 7-year-olds, about a fifth for 9-year-olds, and a quarter for 11-year-olds. It is important to remember that these were not items chosen by HMI as being necessary. They were chosen because, individually, they were thought worth including by 80 per cent of the teachers. Two items appeared universally, at least for an age group. Reading practice with a book from a reading scheme took place in every class with 7-year-olds (i.e. the oldest infants). Every class of each age group practised sums.

The supposition that teachers no longer cared to teach children to read and to calculate was plainly false. Tests carried out by the NFER in parallel with the survey provided objective evidence about the mathematical ability of 11-year-olds and about reading for 9- and 11-year-olds. For the most part that information was useful within the survey in making comparisons between sub-groups and between specific findings. The reading tests for 11-year-olds was the rather dated NS6 which had the advantage that it had been used nationally in 1955, 1960 and 1970. The mean score had increased between 1955 and 1960 but fell by 0.1 to 29.38 in 1970. That fall was the trigger that gave rise to the Bullock Committee. In 1976/7 the mean score had risen to 31.13 and the statistician comparing the results over the whole series concluded that it could be said 'with confidence that the data . . . were consistent with a rising trend in reading standards . . . '. That is not at all the same thing as saying that they are good enough for the circumstances in which children are and will later find themselves, nor that they are as good as the children can achieve. The other tests had not been used in national surveys previously and so comparisons could not be made with past results.

Basics Versus the Rest

So far from under-teaching what are often called the basics — reading, writing and arithmetic — as some[19] outside primary schools alleged, teachers continued to give these aspects of their work high priority. The results of national surveys seem to indicate that 11-year-olds have become more rather than less competent readers on average. Many primary schools used time-tables which gave over the mornings to the basics and the afternoons to the rest. Of course the practice was never as simple nor as universal as this generalization suggests.

Even so, the HMI surveys of First and 8–12 Middle Schools[20] and the studies undertaken in the ORACLE Project[21] confirmed the general condition, though the first two recorded some increase in the teaching of observational and experimental science. Recent published reports by HMI on individual schools indicate that there still is a concentration on teaching children to read, write and do mathematics (the shift of terminology from arithmetic is deliberate), but too often the skills are taught in isolation and gains are lost that would come if the skills were applied in a variety of circumstances.

The condition persuaded Robin Alexander[22] to conclude, with reservations about the dangers of over-simplification, that it might be sensible to speak of two curricula for primary schools: the basics and the rest. In practice, the former has high status and high priority, and the latter as revealed by the HMI surveys and the ORACLE research, is much more closed than it appears at first sight and typically consists of 'undemanding, stultifying topic work' for which the actual choices open to the children are restricted and mundane.

Towards a Unified Curriculum

The question of whether there should be two curricula, and if so in what balance, is fundamental to the future of primary education. To use a different but apposite image, should primary education finally emerge from the elementary education system which is its labouring mother? The criticism from outside primary education — and from a few inside about *other* peoples' alleged practices — often centres on the argument that teaching the basics, i.e. elementary education, is what matters to children's future development and that greater attention than now should be paid to them. My impression is that nearly every primary school teacher would agree that it would be advantageous and even that it is necessary for children to become more literate and more numerate. In my view it is both foolish and wrong for anyone concerned with primary education to behave defensively in response to a demand for improvement in children's learning in these connections. The important question is: how can they be achieved?

The 1978 HMI report[23] on primary schools concluded: 'The teaching of skills in isolation, whether in language or in mathematics, does not produce the best results.' Many HMI surveys and reports on the work of individual schools have expressed disappointment that the isolation continues and continues to be disadvantageous. The requirement, in regard to the basics, is not to reduce the time spent upon them so that something else can be done, nor to increase the time spent on isolated exercises. It is to use the activities that go on throughout the day to improve children's power over language, oral and written, and whenever opportunity occurs or is made, to improve their range and skills in mathematics.

That proposition is not aimed at diminishing further the status or priority of the 'other' curriculum. On the contrary more thought, not less, needs to be given to the range and depth of skills, ideas and attitudinal values that can be increased through the studies and activities, the topics, that are the centres of attention.

A Framework for Thinking

Part of the difficulty in the day-to-day practice of teaching — or in inspecting the work of a class — is to carry a mental framework that will allow an 'on the hoof' assessment of what is being done. The assessment is vital in deciding what should be done next. There are so many concepts and skills that should be introduced, extended or refined and so kept in mind. What follows is no more than one arrangement that has been useful to me in watching and listening to children and thinking about what might come next.

Concepts

Much of what is done in developing children's ideas of the world around them can be considered from four main viewpoints:

(a) *discrimination*: throughout their learning children have to notice how things that they previously thought to be much the same or to differ in indiscriminate, meaningless ways, actually differ according to set criteria which operate again and again. Whatever the children are currently doing, we can ask whether they should be discriminating more finely or through the use of additional criteria. There is probably an infinite variety of examples, and I shall take four types to illustrate the range:

i. of the vast number of examples from learning to read, write and do mathematics — distinguishing p from q; disinterested from uninterested; when to read slowly and carefully and when to skip; 38,000 from threethousand eight-hundred (sic); area from length (something a lot of adults have difficulty with);

ii. to recognize whether an approach is aggressive or fearful; supportive or undermining;

iii. to separate metals that can be magnetized from others that cannot be; or the one variable to be tested from others that should be kept constant;

iv. to choose which course of action or which tool is likely to be most productive in the circumstances.

Although, potentially, the possibilities are endless, in practice they are limited by the prevailing conditions.

(b) *classification and generalization*: in many ways the obverse of discrimination and probably brought less to primary school children's attention, though just as important. Again the examples are infinite in number and vast in range, but whatever the children are doing the question can be posed: should they be helped to be more aware of the underlying similarities between what may appear to be different items or events, or the consistency of a pattern half-revealed? For example:

i. writing a, c, d, g, o, or q, all require the same anti-clockwise movement to start with;

ii. people tend to use local materials when building shelter from the elements;

iii. squares are two-dimensional figures with four straight sides of equal length, joining at right angles, differing in position and possibly in size, but not in shape;

iv. the idea of acceptable limits or tolerance has application in a variety of human activities including social behaviour, measurement, quality control of ingredients;

v. changes in motion require transfer of energy.

Classes of things may themselves be hierarchical. There are many children (and adults) who think that only mammals, but not themselves, are animals: they have not yet learnt that people are a subset of mammals, mammals are a subset of animals. At the boundaries between classes there are commonly individual cases that may be assigned to one or the other only with difficulty and even arbitrarily.

(c) *inter-relations*: to what extent are children learning to recognize that actions produce reactions or consequences, though they may not always be easy to trace? For example

i. in most cases, as something gets warmer it expands, though there are some interesting exceptions;

ii. if the diameter of one circle is twice as long as the diameter of another, the area of its circle is four times bigger;

iii. there is an optimum amount of water to use when modelling clay, too much and it collapses, too little and it cracks and is difficult to shape;

iv. when people, over the years, walk up and down a spiral staircase they wear a depression in the steps in the form of a skewed parabola.

(Perhaps I should say that I have chosen all the examples, including the last, from among those I have seen being investigated by primary school children.)

(d) *symbolization and representation*: in order to be able to use and build on experience, children need to encapsulate it in ways that allow it to be recalled, mulled over and applied. Language is the paramount medium for most people for most of the time, but the number system, algebra, diagrams and maps, pictures and models, music, mime and other forms of movement, even some games, all contribute. The representations may relate to what is understood to be 'factual' information, but they may also express feelings and provide explanations, whether based on observation or conjectured. The symbols may themselves be used to create systems, for example in arithmetic, algebra and surrealism.

Skills

Skills are difficult to define. For the present purposes they are aspects of behaviour that can be carried out semi-automatically, though to do so may require practice and occasionally close, sustained attention may have to be given.

Six kinds of development to be looked for as children go through primary schools are:

(a) the range of skills a child can call on should be being extended;

(b) a child should increasingly be able to apply the skills with an *appropriate* degree of control and precision, i.e. not always more precision;

(c) and with increased strength where that is appropriate;

(d) he or she should increasingly be able to choose the appropriate skill or sub-skill for the current purpose;

(e) as part of (a) to (d), a child should be able to select from and use a wider range of appropriate tools, instruments and apparatus as he or she matures;

(f) as a consequence, some of the skills developed become more complex in operation.

Some skills are concerned with interpreting or enhancing the messages coming in from the outside; others are concerned with delivering messages or shaping/modifying one's circumstances. They obviously include skills related to language, including the use of conventions that enable the receiver to pay attention to the meaning of what is said or written and not be disconcerted by idiosyncratic or (to the receiver) unconventional forms or expressions. Handwriting, syntax and spelling, on that count, should be thought of pragmatically as necessary ways of getting one's message across rather than being elevated to matters of status or principle. 'Correct' language is, in the terms of the Bullock Report,[24] language that is right for the circumstances. Skill in using numbers, measuring, weighing, setting out algorithms, drawing and interpreting graphs, maps and diagrams all require attention. As do the abilities to use pencil, pen, paintbrush, scissors, knife, drill, that will shape the line, the area of paint, the paper, the wood or perhaps plastic, or the gluebrush, adhesive, nail, screw, peg, shaped joint or solder that will fasten parts together. All children should learn to use percussion and tonal instruments as well as to sing.

The children need to learn to read a variety of scales for measuring length, capacity, area; and to use magnifying glasses, microscopes (particularly binocular microscopes), tape recorders, radios, television sets, binoculars, telescopes, cameras to observe and record what they might not otherwise see. All should be familiar with the use of calculators and with microcomputers.

Attitudes

In some ways, attitudinal changes are the most difficult effects of education to describe developmentally. It has been said again and again that children should learn to become increasingly independent, and of course they should. They should also learn more about the extent to which they depend upon the efforts of others, many of whom they will never meet. They should learn to become more persistent, carrying an activity through to its conclusion. But they should also learn when it is sensible to change tack, and not to waste energy and resources pursuing what is, at least for the time being, unachievable. Children should learn to be more tolerant, yet not to tolerate cruelty or racism or sexism. They should learn to be honest, but not, in all cases, to be determined to tell the whole truth no matter how much it hurts the listener. They should learn to respect their fellows, but not that part of a fellow that cheats or bullies.

The message is intriguingly like that of the Bullock Committee on language: what is appropriate is what suits the circumstances. Life would be simpler if there were clear cut answers, but there are not. Perhaps one aspect of maturity that education should foster is that children should gradually become less inclined to react instantaneously but rather to count to ten before deciding what to do, though even that is inappropriate in some circumstances.

Bringing the Elements Together

The concepts, skills and attitudes operate and grow in a context of social interaction and a flow of information about people, animals, plants and the non-living world. Figure 2.1 has been helpful to me when thinking about what teachers and children are doing, and could be useful in deciding what aspects of children's learning should be advanced in undertaking an activity or topic:

Figure 2.1

	Skills	Concepts	Attitudes
People			
Plants and animals		Activities	
Materials		and topics	

Obviously, one activity or topic will call on different inform-ation, skills, concepts and attitudes from another, and in a different balance. To take one aspect, information about people may be concerned with what people believe, what they have done, what they imagine, with the explanations they provide and feelings they express. Factual information shades into fantasy. Some groups are beginning to use much the same grid/diagrammatic approach to bring coherence to the separate subject statements on the National Curriculum.[25] At their best, standard assessment tasks produced for the National Curriculum will provide more examples, but many are required so that teachers may build up a collection, many of which may be of their own making with particular children and local circumstances in mind. If that does not happen, the new curriculum will be less tailor-made for the children than it should be.

Notes

1. Blenkin, G. M. and Kelly, A. V. (Eds) (1983) *The Primary Curriculum in Action*, Chapter 1, London, Harper and Row.
2. Rowland, S. (1984) *The Enquiring Classroom*, Lewes, The Falmer Press.
3. Armstrong, M. (1980) *Closely Observed Children*, London, Writer and Readers.
4. Warnock, H. M. (1978) *Meeting Special Educational Needs*, London, HMSO.
5. Joseph, Sir Keith, Secretary of State for Education and Science (6 January 1984): speech to the North of England Conference, Sheffield.
6. DES/WO (1977) Cmnd. 6869, pp. 6–7, London, HMSO.
   DES/WO (1980) *A Framework for the School Curriculum*, London, HMSO.
   DES/WO (1981) *The School Curriculum*, p. 3, London, HMSO.
   DES/WO (1985) *Better Schools*, p. 14, London, HMSO.
7. DES (1981) *Circular 6/81*.
8. Northamptonshire LEA (1983) *Principles for the Primary Curriculum*, p. 7, Northampton, Northamptonshire County Council.
9. Northamptonshire LEA (1985) *The School Curriculum. A Framework of Principles*, Northampton, Northamptonshire County Council.
10. DES/WO (1985) *Better Schools, op. cit.*, p. 20.
11. See Chapter 4 for a fuller description of the Schools Council.
12. Mackay, D. (1969 and following) *Breakthrough to Literacy*, London, Longman.

Ennever, L. and Harlen, W. (1972) *With Objectives in Mind: Guide to Science 5–13*, London, MacDonald Educational.

Tough, J. (1977) *Talking and Learning: A Guide to Fostering Communication Skills in Nursery and Infant Schools*, London, Ward Lock.

13. Ashton, P. M. E., Kneen, P., Davies, F. and Holly, B. J. (1975) *Aims of Primary Education: A Study of Teachers' Opinions*, London, University of London Press.

14. Schools Council Working Paper 70 (1981) *The Practical Curriculum*, London, Methuen Educational.

15. Schools Council (1983) *Primary Practice*, London, Methuen.

16. DES/HMI (1980) *A View of the Curriculum*, London, HMSO; (see also Chapter 6).

17. DES/HMI (1978) *Primary Education in England*, London, HMSO.

18. *ibid.*, pp. 77–79.

19. Cox, C. B. and Dyson, A. E. (Eds) (1969–1977) *Black Papers*, London, The Critical Quarterly Society.

20. DES/HMI (1982) *Education 5–9: an Illustrative Survey of 80 First Schools in England*, London, HMSO.
DES/HMI (1985) *Education 8–12 in Combined and Middle Schools*, London, HMSO.

21. Galton, M. and Simon, B. (Eds) (1980) *Progress and Performance in the Primary Classroom*, London, Routledge and Kegan Paul.
Galton, M., Simon, B. and Croll, P. (1980) *Inside the Primary Classroom*, London, Routledge and Kegan Paul.

22. Alexander, R. J. (1984) *Primary Teaching*, Eastbourne, Holt Education.

23. DES/HMI (1978) *Primary Education in England*, *op. cit.*, p. 112.

24. DES (1975) Bullock Report, *op. cit.*

25. ASE, ATM, MA, NATE (1989) *The national curriculum, making it work for the primary school*, Hatfield, Association for Science Education.

Chapter 3

The Curriculum: The Main Subdivisions

The children need to know everything, including some things that we cannot yet guess! If we are to make sensible choices in what to bring to children's notice or to select from what they may propose, then we have to have a sense of the whole and distinguish major aspects of the curriculum. The traditional divisions are the subjects whose names have become familiar on timetables, but they are not the only possible sub-divisions.

An HMI Model

HM Inspectorate used a different form of analysis in *Curriculum Matters 2*,[1] though supplementary publications deal with the subjects one by one. The basic document proposed nine areas of experience: aesthetic and creative; human and social; linguistics and literacy; mathemetical; moral; physical; scientific; spiritual; and technological. The writers then identified four elements: knowledge; concepts; attitudes and skills, the last being divided into communication, observation, study, problem solving, physical and practical, creative and imaginative, numerical and personal and social. The following specific issues were thought worth highlighting: environmental; health education; information technology; political education; education in economic understanding; preparation for work; careers; equal opportunities; the multi-cultural nature of society. To Sir Keith Joseph's four principles were added progression and continuity.

The areas of experience had been worked out in the 1970s in a cooperative exercise with secondary schools. There is an obvious link between the areas of experience discussed by HMI and the aspects of thinking as described earlier by Hirst and Peters.[2] As Hirst has pointed out, some of the forms of thinking he identified, like the mathematical, have close associations with subjects that appear on school (or class) timetables. Other timetabled subjects, like geography, call on a number of ways of thinking and so the association between the two sets of categories is only partial. The 'specific issues' in the HMI document look like topical interests that children should be informed about, and are no worse for being that: perhaps current concern should be one of the criteria for the selection of material to be included.

The model has the advantage that it makes it possible to think about the curriculum at a more fundamental level than the timetable.

The Traditional School Subjects

The Hadow (1931) and Plowden (1967) Reports both discussed the curriculum under subject headings. It is interesting to compare the lists:

Hadow	*Plowden*
Religious Education	Religious Education
English including reading	English including reading
	Modern languages
History	History
Geography	Geography
Arithmetic and simple geometry	Mathematics
The Study of Nature	Science
Music	Music
Drawing and elementary art	Art and Craft
Handwriting	
Handicraft	
Physical Training and Games	Physical Education

Health Education   Sex education
Corporate Life and the
 Training of Character

The last two in the Hadow list were described as being 'given indirectly as an integral part of the daily life of the school' and as being the subject of 'short talks' and influenced by 'the school and its general environment'.[3] The Plowden Report had a separate section on relationships in primary schools, touching on the same issues as Hadow's final section.

The Plowden Report, in earlier paragraphs,[4] discussed the role of play and the place of activity and experience in shaping what is done in schools. It referred to Hadow's much quoted sentence: 'the curriculum is to be thought of in terms of activity and experience rather than of knowledge to be acquired and facts to be stored.' It put that back into its context, which recognized that learning could also take place from imaginative experience, and that the acquisition of knowledge and facts is and should be an outcome of activity and experience. The issue is obviously a difficult one to grasp, for in the course of this section[5] Plowden coined one of the sentences for which it is most famous, but which often has its meaning twisted by misquotation: 'The child is the agent in [not '*of*', NT] his own learning.' The word 'play' carries its own difficulties. To many people it means 'playing about' and that is not what it should mean in the education of young children — though there is a place for playing about in life from time to time. Play in the education of young children is more to do with experimentation, imitation and practice and is often rather a serious business for the children. So much is plain when children at a richly endowed water tray use the various tubes and containers to see what they can make the water do, or what it may do; or when children in the classroom shop, hairdresser's or museum act out the interweaving roles of the adults they are pretending to be.

Discussion on the timetable will be taken up in more detail when organization and methodology are the focus, but it is necessary to point out here that the Plowden Report acknowledged 'a revolution from the type of timetable . . . ' which showed 'exactly what each class was doing during every minute of the week', and that children in the same room may, at the same time, be engaged in different sorts of activities. On the other hand, 'the teacher must constantly ensure a balance within the day or week both for the class and for individuals.'[6]

The Subjects of the National Curriculum

Just as Hadow and Plowden fell into the use of subject headings when discussing the primary school curriculum, so has the Secretary of State and Parliament in defining the National Curriculum. The Education Reform Act (ERA) of 1988 listed nine Foundation Subjects for English primary schools, preceded by religious education. The list is set out for easy comparison with the Hadow and Plowden lists:

mathematics
English
science
history
geography
technology
music
art
physical education.

The first three are designated 'core subjects', and Welsh is added as a foundation subject in Wales, being a core subject in Welsh-speaking schools. A modern foreign language is added for children in the second and third key stages (generally for children from 11 to 14, and 14 to 16 years of age). The National Curriculum is not intended to be the whole curriculum, though it is expected to be most of it. It is difficult to understand why the first three (plus Welsh) should be called core subjects unless it is to reassure the public that the Government thinks they matter. Since all are to be compulsory, though with different levels of prescription, they all matter — and should.

Comparing the Hadow, Plowden and ERA lists gives some clues about the ways content has either persisted or changed over the years. Religious education is present in all, though it is not a foundation subject of the National Curriculum. English, history, geography, music, physical education (with games in the Hadow Report) appear in all three lists. The arithmetic and simple geometry of Hadow become transformed into mathematics, and the study of nature changes to science in both Plowden and ERA. Drawing/elementary art and handicraft become first art and craft and then, separately, art and technology, with substantially different intentions for the latter. Health education becomes sex education and then is left out, though there has been considerable recent debate on both: concerning the first as a 'cross-curricular' matter and the latter according to the responsibility of school governors in deciding on its inclusion. Handwriting appeared in Hadow but not later. Corporate life and character training were a concern of Hadow and personal relations an interest of Plowden. Modern languages appeared in Plowden but in neither of the others for primary schools.

Of course there have been changes in content, methodology and balance in the teaching of those subjects whose names have remained constant. There is no doubt in my mind that children listen, speak, read and write in more ways and, at least in the last three, more often now than they did even in 1967, taking schools as a whole. The Bullock Report (1975)[7] has stimulated that development, as has the National Writing Project[8] more recently. History and geography have probably been more affected by changes of methodology than content since 1967, though there have been changes in content over sixty years, with social history coming more to the fore than political history, and some local or newer industries, like oil and electricity, replacing fishing and mining in many schools as matters of interest. Immediate and current events, like the Olympics or major disasters, have focused attention on places that do not make regular appearances in primary school work. Themes like transport or dress or housing may combine geographical and historic interests. There have been many and worrying complaints, for example from HMI, that the choice of topics is too idiosyncratic, each being worked in isolation from what went before and what is to come, and with little nsideration given to what skills, concepts and attitudes are to be fostered as a result of the study.

Some Disadvantages of Single Forms of Curricular Analysis

The difficulty of producing any single list of discrete categories that describe the primary school curriculum is apparent in the HMI analysis and hidden in the subject analysis only because of its familiarity. The subconscious belief that it is possible to produce an all-embracing list has implications for the ways in which some teaching has been organized and has directly affected the teaching of some important skills.

The Notion of Integration

A lot of energy has been expended in the last thirty years discussing whether a subject-based approach is right in primary schools, generally in order to reach the conclusion that it is not. Small children, it has been argued, do not think in subject terms, hence the popularity of the use of topic or thematic approaches. In secondary schools there has been a parallel discussion, with some arguing for bringing subjects together in what has been called an integrated approach, and the idea of integration has been advocated for primary schools, though the term *integrated* has also been used to describe a form of organization in which different kinds of activity — it could even be different subjects — are pursued by different groups of children in a class at the same time. For the present I shall use *integration* to refer to aspects of the curriculum and not to the organization of a class.

The Plowden Report was criticized by some teachers who were disappointed that it discussed the curriculum in subject terms while advocating a more subject-integrated approach to teaching. The Bullock Report went as far as to advocate that English should be taught 'across the curriculum'.

There is, I suggest, a confusion between discussing and deciding upon the curriculum on the one hand and organizing the teaching and learning on the other. If those two are kept separate, as they should be, there is no discord in the Plowden Report. There is confusion in the Bullock Report,[9] which would have provided a clearer message if it had advocated that due attention should be given to the pupils' use of English no matter when it occurred in the *timetable*: whatever the lesson, the concern is still with English.

The confusion between discussing the curriculum and operating it has led to an unhelpfully rigid stance being taken against the idea of curricular subjects in connection with primary education. The fact is that even the youngest children do engage in activities that are clearly single-subject dominated. They are brought together to listen to a story: English. They sing and play musical instruments. They go as a class to engage in physical education in the hall, playground or on the school field it it has one. If not as a class, as individuals they spend time on art: painting a picture; or craft: making a model. Of course, while they are doing those things they listen and talk, they learn to share and to take turns, they may read, they may even count. None of the activites is purely single-subject, and nor will they be when they are carried out in the secondary school and the lessons are given subject names.

Children also engage in things that are difficult to identify by any one subject name, though it would certainly be possible to identify some subjects within them. A topic they are following may encompass historical, geographical and scientific aspects. For example, it may centre on the study of a hedgerow. The children may be engaged in learning about the plants and animals to be found; they may set up experiments to test out their assumptions as to why certain growth patterns occur in plants on the northern side of the hedge and others on the southern side. Perhaps they will make and set small mammal traps. They may undertake some surveying so that the hedge can be mapped, and compare their mapping with large scale Ordnance Survey maps, present and past. They may collect information about the age of the hedge and what was happening locally, and perhaps nationally, at various times in its history. They will certainly talk, write, read books, draw pictures, diagrams and graphs, and paint to record what they have found out, and they may well have to understand and apply some mathematics in the surveying, sampling, measuring and making. If the work is well arranged, they should have learnt a bit more about how and when to operate in a group and when alone. When the activity is picked apart and separate aspects (possibly taking place simultaneously) allocated according to traditional subject headings, it becomes clear that a number of 'subjects' have been touched upon. The topic is said to be one in which the subjects have been integrated.

The best one can say about the primary school operation of the curriculum is that attention is sometimes focused on an activity that could reasonably be given a subject name, and at other times not. What matters is that the focus stimulates the learning that is being sought. I think we have worried all too much about the subject: topic dichotomy as though one approach was right and the other wrong.

Indeed, the word *integration* signals that an adult view rather than a child's view is being expressed: a backwards perspective rather than a forwards perspective. What needs to be acknowledged is that children will be helped, as they learn more, if they can develop a way of categorizing knowledge just as a librarian classifies books. To do that they have to step back a little from their immediate interest and think about the characteristics of the subject itself. We should help children to take on studies such as that of the hedgerow, as ways of learning more about their environment and also draw attention, more and more as the children mature, to the subject categories into which their learning can be sorted. The movement should be from the use of undifferentiated (not *integrated*) topics towards a heightened awareness of the variety of knowledge, not the process of trying to stuff all the snakes into one black bag.

The children, like the librarian, would be wise to recognize that even the best system of categorizing knowledge is man-made, not an attribute of nature, and that it sometimes breaks down. The frequency of strongly subject-oriented work is likely to increase as the children get older. As Plowden said, 'As children come to the top of the junior school, and we anticipate they will be there till 12, the conventional subjects become more relevant; some children can then profit from a direct approach to the structure of the subject.'

Constraints Arising From Subject Definitions

Some difficulties arise because unduly strong but questionable links have been forged between certain skills and specific subjects.

The first stages of teaching reading are often linked with writing. Children give an account of something they have been doing, they may draw a picture or make a model, and then, with the teacher's help, write a label or a few words of amplification. Sometimes these pieces of writing are gathered together and used as a reading book.

For the most part, however, the commercially produced books used in the early stages of teaching of reading are still trivial stories that ape literature. The presumption that teaching children to read is part of the English course, and that English is substantially to do with literature (or linguistics for that matter) has created unnecessary and harmful limits on the range of children's early reading. It is at least arguable that the disproportionate number of boys who find learning to read difficult would be reduced if children were given earlier and more opportunities to read non-fiction, including instructions, recipes and descriptions. There is every reason why early reading books should be about and stimulate the range of children's experience inside and outside school. Some parts of that experience, like learning mathematics, provide an excellent setting for the teaching of reading in which the repeated use of the same words and phrases is required by the content, not forced upon it.

Similarly, there is no reason why the teaching of handwriting should be linked uniquely with English. It is a physical skill requiring control over the small muscles of the arm and hand, co-ordination between hand and eye, feeling for place, proportion and rhythm. The skill has as much to do with art and physical education as it has to do with English. Familiarization with the microcomputer keyboard presents a similar problem of placement in a subject.

Difficulties Arising From a Narrowness of Definition

In both geography and history it will be important to develop the

National Curriculum in a way that acknowledges the essential teaching that goes on with the youngest children in school. The work should be planned to promote their understanding of time, place and people — and the associations between them — on a personal level of what happens inside and outside school, and affects children's daily lives. The development of consciousness about the variety of groups to which a child belongs, about the suitability of some activities to some places and not others, about family histories and ramifications are all essential to the growth of a wider understanding of relationships between people and their circumstances and the ways in which they change over time. Understanding and tolerance of the rights of others in the class and one's own responsibilities are a necessary base for the development of racial and religious tolerance and an acceptance of social obligations. They are just as much a part of education for adult life as are learning about the foundations of the Parliamentary system and our dependence on World trade. The children in the well-arranged nursery area were learning about the relationship between place and activity when they moved from the wet and messy area with its taps, bowls, hard and easily cleaned surfaces, where they painted and made models, to the softer, more muted and relaxing quiet area for the mid-morning story: the more they are made conscious of the relation between surroundings and activity the more easily they will learn to appreciate the relation between the climatic and geophysical circumstances in which a group of people live and the activities in which they engage.

A Mixture of Models

If the arguments here are accepted, there is a case for using subject divisions of knowledge for the purposes of the National Curriculum. Certainly the use is not worth campaigning against, providing those operating the system do not turn the convenience into a straightjacket. Indeed, when tracking through from the emergence of school subjects to the formation of courses in higher education it becomes obvious that the actual subjects as taught have to change and sometimes re-combine: broad observation, enquiry and manipulation lead into general science which breaks down into physics, chemistry and biology; these subdivisions may then re-combine to form biochemistry and also contribute to cybernetics, ecology, public health and so on, which call on knowledge outside science.

The fact is that there is not a logical, coherent, tidy, all-embracing way of analyzing and describing the curriculum. If that is remembered then the subject division can provide a tool for some descriptive purposes, to be turned and abused to fit the non-conformist elements when they occur. It was acceptable, for example, for the English Working Group on the National Curriculum[10] to deal with reading and with handwriting provided no-one supposed that what they had to say would be more than a part of what is to be said on the matters. In fact, since the art, physical education and even geography and history groups were nowhere in sight at the time of the formation of the English Working Group, it was necessary that someone should pick up such vital curricular interests of primary schools and remind everyone of their importance. Unfortunately, in taking up an interest in handwriting, the English Working Group, and now the Statutory Orders, make the mistake of combining writing for meaning, spelling and handwriting in a single profile component for assessment purposes. It is difficult to imagine why it should be supposed to be reasonable to give a single judgement about the three, for ability in one is neither a requirement nor any necessary guide to ability in either of the others. The need is to use the headings in ways that will promote what is required in children's learning but not allow them to diminish the range, relevance, differentiation and balance of what is taught. Nor should the headings be allowed to dominate the methodology used in teaching. The requirement is that the teaching is effective in producing the required learning, not that it must be split, always, according to the headings.

Inside schools, the HMI analysis will still be useful when planning and constructing activities, and it is positively advantageous, in my view to use one curricular model to construct the curriculum and another to review it. In that way any missing parts or loose connections between the aspects used for construction become apparent in the review. In effect, two different sieves are used.

Notes

1. DES/HMI (1985) *The Curriculum from 5 to 16, Curriculum Matters 2*, London, HMSO.
2. Hirst, P. H. and Peters, R. S. (1970) *The Logic of Education*, London, Routledge and Kegan Paul.
   Hirst, P. H. (1974) *Knowledge and the Curriculum*, London, Routledge and Kegan Paul.
3. Board of Education (1931) Hadow Report, pp. 201–203, London, HMSO.
4. DES (1967) Plowden Report, paragraphs 523ff., London, HMSO.
5. DES (1967) Plowden Report, paragraph 529, *op. cit.*
6. DES (1967) Plowden Report, paragraph 537, *op. cit.*
7. DES (1975) Bullock Report, London, HMSO.
8. Schools Curriculum Development Committee (1987) *The National Writing Project*; materials to be published by Thomas Nelson, Walton on Thames.
9. DES (1975) Bullock Report, *op. cit.*
10. DES/WO (1988) *English for Ages 5 and 11*, Subject Working Party chaired by C. B. Cox, London, HMSO.

Chapter 4

Who Determines the Curriculum?

A Period of Government Reticence

For a time after 1944, Ministers were careful not to express views on what schools should be doing. George Tomlinson was very highly regarded as the Minister in 1950. Speaking to a course organized by Hertfordshire for its Education Committee, he referred to the opening clause of the 1944 Education Act, which gave power to the Minister to control the education of the country, and said: 'I think that's a wonderful thing so long as the Minister never does it.'[1]

The presumption was that the curriculum should be decided by teachers. Life was never so simple nor control anywhere near so absolute. It was not clear who the teachers were, but in any disagreement it was much more likely to be the headteacher than the classteacher who chose the way forward. Certainly some classteachers were asked to produce schemes of work which might be discussed at staff meetings, though these meetings were not so common or held so frequently as in the 1980s. The headteacher would still take the final decisions about what to include.

Some External Influences on The Curriculum

If individual preference were the whole story, then it would be difficult to explain why there was such a similarity in the curriculum from school to school in the late 1940s and early 1950s. There have always been at least four important sources of influence in addition to the more institutional ones that are discussed later.

Tradition

One was tradition. Although the system of payment by results and a laid down curriculum was virtually ended by 1896, the shape of the timetable and a considerable part of the content persisted for decades and in a substantial number of schools right up to the mid-1960s. Although, in the Plowden Report, it was possible to write of changes in the teaching of geography, for example, that had led to a steady increase in outdoor work in the last 20 or 30 years, it was also necessary to say that 'schools today show an enormous variation' in the use of their localities. A school at 'the head of the procession has advanced far beyond the tail'.[2] In mathematics there was hardly any change in content, which continued to be mainly arithmetic, mental and written, with some calculations arrived at through imaginary shopping or agricultural expeditions. The simple geometry was most often concerned with calculating the areas of rectangles. The weekly composition traced the adventures of a wayward penny or recounted a story previously read by the teacher or the better readers in the class. Nevertheless, as the geographers noticed, there was movement. *The Story of a School*,[3] published in 1949, was written by its headteacher, A. L. Stone, who subsequently became a powerful influence in the local inspectorate of the West Riding LEA, and more widely. It tells of the transformation of a downtown Birmingham junior school, brought about mainly by development in the teaching of art and dance. Children's new freedom to express themselves, where it occurred, was largely due to changes in the teachers' expectations and attitudes, but also stimulated by a wider range of tools and opportunities to develop ideas. Even so, in arithmetic,

> we introduced all methods of practical work . . . but I could withal not convince myself that this method was giving the child the reality which was necessary for his development through this subject. The 'C' child inevitably found difficulty in adding $2\frac{1}{2}$d. and $3\frac{1}{2}$d. together in his head in these circumstances, but he would buy stamps of the same value from the post office and be sure to get the right change.

The choice of example has its own significance.

Selection for Secondary Education

A second influence was the system, almost everywhere, of distributing children from a primary school to different types of secondary schools: grammar, a few technical, more and more secondary modern, fewer and fewer classes for older children in all-age schools. Various arrangements were made, and still are made where selection occurs, to separate the children into two main groups, or three where technical schools existed. In some areas the divisions were and are into more groups as the most prestigious of the local grammar schools makes its first claim on next year's entry. Two main systems of selection have been used, often in combination: the results of tests chosen by the LEA; and teachers' opinions about the suitability of each child for grammar school education. Some will cavil at that description, and prefer to talk of suitability for either grammar school or secondary modern school education. Even where teachers' opinions were paramount in deciding, the teachers often gave considerable weight to the results of tests, usually standardized tests in arithmetic and reading, conducted within the school. What else was there to stand upon, some felt, when a parent accused the school of malice or favouritism?

The result was that the tests used, whether chosen by the LEA or by the school, to some extent constrained what was taught. School reputations were at least thought to be dependent upon the number (hardly even the proportion) of children going on to grammar schools, and so, for some, it was more important that the number of grammar school entrants was high than that the 'right' children went. Perhaps the view was that while it was not too difficult to distinguish between A and Z it was impossible to do so between F and H, so both had better be 'given the chance' of a grammar school education which, after all, was the better resourced. The tests used had all been tried out on groups of earlier pupils to be reasonably sure they contained no nonsenses. That earlier proving has the effect of making the tests conservative in form rather than radical. Not only were they, then, something that many thought it right to teach towards, they were also models of what the powers that be, those misty figures, regarded as right. Unlike secondary school teachers who could read the examination syllabuses and learn what might be in store, there was and is no syllabus for the secondary selection examination. At least one primary school went on training its 10-year-olds in the long multiplication and divisions of money including farthings for at least three years after farthings had been discarded as a unit of currency. After all, next year's test might include them as, actually, had the test used in the year following their demise.

Many have regretted what they regard as a resultant over-concentration on exercises in English comprehension and arithmetic or, more recently, mathematics. Others say that the existence of the tests provide a goal for a school to work towards and give an edge to its work. My impression is that both views have been overplayed. The move towards non-streaming, the beginnings of the changes in teaching mathematics and the more extreme approaches to 'creative' writing were all well under way before DES Circular 10/65 was drafted asking LEAs to say how they were planning to reorganize secondary education and establish comprehensive schools. What is more, as we shall see shortly, the number of tests being set inside primary schools, often at the insistence of the LEA, has increased since the mid-1960s. Schools do need to be clearheaded about the directions in which they should be taking their pupils, and about the directions in which they are going as institutions, but if the goal is limited to reading and some aspects of mathematics, and mainly concerns the border-area pupils for grammar school selection, then if it were influential its influence would have to be narrowing, and disadvantageous to the progress of most of the pupils in the school, including the quickest in any aspect of learning. If there has been some loss of a sense of pace in primary schools, and I think there may have been, it comes much more from a general shift in relationships within society than from the presence or absence of the 11-plus tests. Getting the pace right is very difficult, as the earlier discussion on 'match' suggested. The problem is to give children a sense of movement and even briskness in their learning, but not haste; and as far as possible to make the pace derive from the task in hand with the deadlines well understood, agreed and even negotiated with the children. That is an important aspect of the High Scope Project[4] being used in some nursery schools and classes; the principle could usefully be adopted more widely.

As *The Story of a School* shows, however, it would be wrong to attribute too much to the influence of the 11-plus examinations. A growing number of schools expanded their range of work outside the fields covered by the examinations, often English 'comprehension', arithmetic and so-called verbal reasoning, earlier called intelligence tests. Even within those fields of work, some schools and their teachers took the view that what best developed their children's general capacities in English language and mathematics also and incidentally helped them when it came to the 11-plus tests. The extra they needed was little more than some familiarity with the styles of the tests, and a sense of haste, which children could acquire in a few practice runs near the date.

Now that children in only a minority of primary schools face the examination it is not easy to tell, from a visit outside the examination period, that their programmes are different in any consistent way from that of schools in areas where the children go to comprehensive schools. It also has to be remembered that in many areas where there is wholly comprehensive secondary schooling, the primary school children have continued to take tests provided by LEAs, including in their final year of primary education. These tests are usually of reading and mathematics. In the ILEA, verbal reasoning tests were set for many years as part of the process of dividing the children into three groups with the intention of ensuring that each comprehensive school had a 'balanced' intake. The ILEA also set tests of reading, English and mathematics.

Resources and Resourcing

A third influence on the work of primary schools was and is the volume, range and style of their resources, especially books. As with many relationships, things are more complicated than they seem at first. In this case they are affected by the funds available to the schools and the supply of ideas available to the publishers and equipment makers, most of the ideas coming from people concerned with primary education, and some of the most effective coming from primary school teachers. The series that changed the content and perhaps the method of teaching history more than anything else was *Looking at History*[5] by R.J. Unstead, a primary school headteacher. One of the points made strongly in *The Story of a School* is that the children were given brushes of different size *to use for the same picture*. Unfortunately, the funding of primary schools has suffered from the historic view that small children cost less: funding has not been calculated according to need. Relatively few schools, and then usually because additional money has been raised from parents, have afforded a binocular microscope or polaroid cameras, both of which are valuable and suitable tools for very young school children, but cost more initially or cost more to run than the less suitable monocular microscope and compact camera which may be afforded, though even they are not in common use.

Schools broadcasting has made a direct and powerful impact on what primary school children do and learn. By the mid-1980s, 98 per cent of primary schools used school broadcasts.[6] They took, on average, 14 series each week. When they are well used, these broadcasts entail preparation and follow-up, so that the total effect on a school's programme is greater than the figures at first suggest. Probably the most influential programmes have been in literature, music, movement, mathematics and science, though many other parts of the curriculum are also included. From time to time the mainstream professional broadcasters have tried to take over the daytime hours allocated to school broadcasts, offering night-time transmission instead. If good recording facilities were provided to primary schools, there would be advantages to the schools as well as to those who propose the changes. It ought to be possible for teachers to view programmes before they are used and the practice ought to be more widespread. It would be easier to manage if the timing of their use was more firmly in each teacher's hand, as it could be with effective, pre-set recording facilities.

Parents and the Community

For most of the period since the passage of the 1944 Education Act the influence of parents on what has been taught has been informal and unsystematic. That is not to say that it has not existed, particularly for articulate people who have been able to put their point of view to heads and teachers and to LEAs and elected members of LEAs. Some parents undoubtedly feel inhibited — justifiably or, much more often, unjustifiably — in telling teachers what they think for fear that the relations between their children and the teachers might suffer. The effect has probably been parental toleration of a wider range of practices rather than to permit a free-for-all.

It is also true that parents are as different from one another as children or teachers, and it is highly unlikely that a teacher could meet the precise wishes of each parent. Parents are too often stereotyped in teachers' discussions, but when the former have sufficient time to expound views, most show that they want much more from schools than that their children learn to read, write and calculate. They do not have a universal view on what the other priorities should be. This one gives first place to children being taught to play musical instruments; that one looks for opportunities in art or drama; the next stresses the importance of multi-cultural or anti-racist education; another emphasises the importance of children becoming familiar with micro-technology and modern means of communication; someone else wants schools to help children to use their leisure well, now and later. All want their children to come willingly to school and virtually all want their children to find learning interesting and worthwhile.[7]

Two interviews with parents stand out particularly in my mind. Both were undertaken in the course of a study of primary education in the ILEA. In the first, the group of parents soon took up the lead provided by one and expressed the view that handwriting was now a neglected subject. They thought it quite inadequate that children should practice handwriting individually from time to time. Everyone in the class should sit down at the same time and be taught. When we met the staff we asked what they did about teaching handwriting. Well, they said, when the children come in from PE they are ready for a quiet sit-down and so we usually take our handwriting lessons then. The point of the story is not to suggest the best way of teaching handwriting, but rather to suggest that teachers may sometimes assume that what they do is so ordinary that parents will know what is happening without being told. The second interview took place with the head of the school present. Only two parents came, though all parents of a class of children had been invited. The two were mothers who, the head told us, hardly ever appeared in school. When they were asked what the most important activity of the school day was, one said that it was certainly the daily story. Her three children slept in the same bed and told each other the stories they had heard during the day. If they hadn't had a story, then the mother told one. The last point was, I thought, the most telling: no matter that she had a pretty tough life, the mother thought that telling stories was well worth making time for. Neither the head nor I would have foreseen the answer to our question. The problem may be to find the time and give the parents the confidence to make their points and ask the questions that interest them.

It is as well for teachers to remember that parents differ from one another and that many teachers are parents. It is also as well to remember that teachers are members of the broader society and so influenced — as variously as other individuals — by the currency of that society.

The Official Channels

The views reported in the previous paragraphs reflect changes in society and in its material circumstances that have a direct bearing on what schools teach. It is not surprising, in an educational system that was without formal, central direction, that different schools came to respond differently in both kind and degree to the changes going on around them. What had, in the main, been a highly conformist provision began to look less so. While it was still possible to recite the traditional subject headings as indicators of what was covered by the curricula of primary schools, the content and also the methodology beneath the headings became more diverse.

But teaching is by nature a conservative rather than a radical profession. The strongest part of a teacher's training is probably that received while a pupil. Only a minority take up teaching because they dislike what they experienced at school and want to change it. Some in the outside world feared that the changes in schools were not keeping pace with the changes outside. It has been widely supposed[8] that the success of the Soviet Union in rocketing a satellite into orbit round the earth caused Western Governments to worry that their education systems were falling behind and should be brought up to date in the content of what they taught, especially mathematics and science. Hardly any of the mathematics taught in schools in the 1950s would have been unfamiliar to Newton, though many new ideas and insights had been developed since his time.

The Curriculum Study Group

In 1960, when he was Minister of Education, Sir David (now Lord) Eccles spoke of the need for his Ministry to enter the 'secret garden of the curriculum' and, two years later, the formation was announced of the Curriculum Study Group, consisting of DES administrators, HMI and 'appropriate experts' from outside.[9] The Group was regarded as a dangerous intrusion by local education authorities and teachers' associations.

The Curriculum Study Groups collaborated with the Nuffield Foundation which funded major curriculum projects including one intended to develop science teaching in primary schools, led by E. R. Wastnedge. Members of the team visited primary schools and shared with the teachers the task of stimulating children's learning, wrote up case studies[10] and produced models that other schools might adapt. Where the team was at work, and in a relatively small number of other schools, the effect was considerable. Primary school children showed themselves capable of sophisticated and prolonged studies when given the right conditions and stimulation. Children in a small village school with a teacher claiming no special training in science carried out a thorough study of a few trees that took them over three years. They kept an account of the variety of animal life sheltered and sustained by the trees. They tried to determine why two trees of the same species flowered at different times. They made a careful estimate of the weight of leaves carried by a broken branch and were surprised by the loss of weight through the drying out of the sample leaves. Where there was sustained support or a teacher who was knowledgeable and confident, the project and the children flowered. It was not successful in affecting the teaching of science nationwide as R. J. Unstead had affected the teaching of history. That is not because the educational value of what was done or produced was inferior, but rather because the intended recipients were not in a position to take and use the material. The simple but difficult lesson for all teachers, whether of children or of adults, is that you must start from where the learners are.

A primary mathematics project,[11] under Geoffrey Matthews, was also set up, but was taken over by the Schools Council. It led to the production of teachers' guides and materials for the children. There can be little doubt that the teaching of mathematics underwent a more radical change than did the teaching of science in the 1960s and 1970s and that the project played an important part.

HM Inspectors of Schools

It did not play the only part, however. It was preceded, paralleled and followed by in-service training directed by Edith Biggs, HMI, who was given the task of influencing the teaching of mathematics in primary schools. She worked principally by running short courses for teacher trainers and for teachers with the help of other HMIs, teacher trainers, LEA advisers and some teachers. Most of the courses lasted the best part of three days. There were sessions on teaching childen how to use numbers, including adding, subtracting, multiplying and dividing; on geometry, including measurement, spatial configurations and relationships, simple surveying; on the application of mathematics, for example to measuring time or testing the strengths of materials. Attention was paid to the ways in which children could represent what they had done by using words, numbers, drawings, graphs, diagrams and models. These aspects were essentially concerned with the methodologies of teaching, though there was some extension beyond traditional content. Later she included material on more recent mathematical ideas like sets and matrices. This example is described at some length because it was probably the most widely known and the most intensive of HMI's activities in the in-service training of teachers, and hence part of the Inspectorate's means of influencing the work of schools. The mathematics programme was by no means the only activity for there has been an annual HMI short course programme for teachers during the whole post-war period. The short courses programme allowed a minority of teachers to pursue a set of ideas at greater length than they otherwise could and, perhaps equally important, provided a relatively neutral meeting place where teachers and HMI could discuss the implications of the practices under review.

DES Programmes and the LEA Training Grants Scheme

The HMI short course programme was and is supplemented by a programme of longer courses in Universities and Colleges. These usually last a term or a year. The cost of replacing teachers while they attended these courses was met from a national pool to which all LEAs contributed. The position has changed since the introduction of the LEA Training Grants Scheme (LEATGS),[12] which is Government funded. More funds are now being made available to schools to choose, within guidelines, their own in-service training programmes. The result has been a fall in the take-up of long courses and, within a remarkably short time, the development of a much greater variety of in-service training, including inter-school visiting. At its best, the new approach has focused more sharply on the needs of individual schools and individual teachers.

As with all teaching and learning, the greatest progress is made by people who are already on the edge of treading into new ground. The people who experience the greatest difficulty are those who catch the excitement, are thrilled — that is not too strong a word in some cases — by what they have done as a result of expert support and tuition, and then find, when they get back to their school, that they are alone with no more than six ideas to last them a year. Too often the principles behind the practice are only partly digested and what is done in the classroom becomes a paper-thin imitation. A good example is the mish-mash of using personal units like the stride and handspan to measure length intermingled with the use of standard units such as the metre; the object of using non-standard units is to help children appreciate the need for widely accepted and common standards. Except for an occasional personal convenience when there is no standard ruler handy, there is no sense in using personal measurements once the need for standard units has been grasped.

The Local Authority Advisory Services

The strength of the LEA advisory services has differed considerably from one LEA to another, though less so since local government re-organization in 1974. The inspectorate in central London, first under the London County Council then from 1965 under the Inner London Education Authority, was a powerful force both before and after the 1944 Education Act. Some of its pre-war members, notably Marion Richardson, are still an influence on what is done in primary schools in England and elsewhere. The West Riding Inspectorate under the general leadership of the Chief Education Officer, (Sir) Alec Clegg, was highly effective in extending the quality and range of primary school children's work in language, dance and art. Edith Moorhouse, officially an assistant education officer with responsibility for primary education, was pre-eminent in developments in Oxfordshire, though with considerable support and his own form of educational leader-ship from Robin Tanner, HMI. Art and light crafts and writing were probably the main curricular areas of development in Oxfordshire primary schools, but as in the West Riding, which had also been influenced by HMIs Christian Schiller's and Robin Tanner's ideas, the emphasis was on the close observation of natural things and often upon constraint rather than flamboyance in art, and on building up a vocabulary of movement or of images that could be used expres-sively. Many schools developed great care and high standards in dis-playing children's work. In Bristol, Marianne Parry's work with teachers of nursery and infant children had substantial effects on their expectations and standing. All of those mentioned and many others carried the same conviction that children should be treated as people, their ideas and efforts respected, and their wish to learn recognized. In Staffordshire, Leicestershire and more widely, Harold Fletcher and Leonard Sealey led headteachers, teachers and others in the advisory services in changing the teaching of mathematics. To name a few inspectors is to appear to disregard the work of dozens of others. To name a few teachers would be to seem to disregard the work of hundreds.

The Schools Council

The Schools Council was set up in 1964 as a result of the disquiet caused by the existence of the Curriculum Study Group. (Lady Plowden and her Central Advisory Council for Education (England) had by then been sitting for a year.) It was seen as a 'hopeful act of reconciliation between central and local government and teachers'.[13] Derek Morrell, the secretary of the Curriculum Study Group was also the greatest single influence on the original shape of the Schools Council. He and Robert Morris, HMI, became the first joint secretaries to the Council. Until 1978, its committees had a majority of teachers; LEAs, DES administrators and HMI made up the greater part of the rest of the membership. The 1978 changes put more direct power into the hands of the LEAs and DES, and extended membership outside the education service, for parents, CBI and TUC. John Mann became the first permanent secretary and John Tomlinson took over as chairman from Sir Alex Smith, who had overseen the review. A view was worked out that provided a framework for deciding on the main areas to be tackled and a system of programmes of operation replaced the concentration on major, but largely one-off, projects. The programmes were:

purpose and planning in school;

helping individual teachers to become more effective;

developing the curriculum for a changing world/developing

basic skills and preparing for life after school;

individual pupils, identifying talents and needs, responding to problems and dealing with difficulties;

improving the examination system.

Among the principles declared to underlie the programmes were a determination to support local curriculum developments, and this was managed through the Morrell Fund, named in honour of the first joint secretary.

As is evident with hindsight, the Schools Council took too long to establish a curricular framework for its operations, so making it more difficult to decide what its priorities should be. It was also a child of its time. There was a mood for change far wider than that affecting the education service, and appearing to move forward often seemed more important than actually moving forward. Actual movement necessitated spending time and money on carrying a project through to its widespread use in schools. The 5–13 science project[14] was an example of a thorough, well thought out piece of work. It took over the baton from the Nuffield Primary Science project, but it needed far more post-development than it had if teachers were to incorporate the practices and ideas espoused; most primary school teachers, then even more than now, lacked confidence in their ability to teach science. One might guess that primary school teachers would not lack confidence in teaching topic work of the historical and geographical kind, yet there was an equally disappointing take-up of the advice contained in the published materials emanating from the Place, Time and Society project.[15] As Harry Rée is reported to have said in the early 1970s: 'for goodness sake put more resources into dissemination, if necessary at the expense of new projects'.[16]

The validity of his plea was not in the slightest diminished by the establishment throughout the country of Teachers' Centres. Often set up in disused school buildings, many were led by a Teachers' Centre Warden who reported to a local committee consisting mainly of teachers and frequently with an LEA adviser or inspector sitting in. They agreed on an annual programme which enabled teachers to meet together and to take part in evening or day courses funded by LEAs. They usually established libraries which included Schools Council publications and a workshop, with tools and equipment for producing teaching materials. But there was no effort or intention by the Council to coordinate the activities of the Teachers' Centres, and no doubt any attempt to do so would have been strenuously resisted by the teachers' associations and by the LEAs.

An outside review of the Schools Council by Nancy Trenaman was conducted in 1981. She made a number of recommendations, including the abolition of the subject committees, but concluded that if the Schools Council did not exist then something like it would have to be invented. If that was the view taken by the Secretary of State (then Sir Keith Joseph) he gave it a radical twist on 22nd April, 1982, when he announced to the House of Commons his intention to disband the Council. That intention was finally effected in March, 1984. Insofar as the Council was replaced, it was replaced by the Secondary Examinations Council, which began its operations in March, 1983, and, separately, with the Schools Curriculum Development Committtee (SCDC) which met first in January, 1984. The latter was given the limited task of identifying gaps, helping to fill them, and assisting with the dissemination of curriculum innovation. The division between the curriculum and examinations/assessment has persisted under the 1988 Education Reform Act in the establishment of the National Curriculum Council and the School Examinations and Assessment Council.

The Schools Council showed, sadly as much by default as by action, that the curriculum should be thought about as a whole so that its parts can be kept in balance. It should be thought of in the context not just of schools, teachers and children, but also in broad social terms. Much of what needs to be done in changing schools' curricula is fine tuning rather than the composition of clarion calls. The latter, unfortunately, appeal to those having to justify large budgets — though the fine tuning may actually cost more. The decisions that have to be made are as often, perhaps more often, about what not to do yet as about which step can now be taken. People making the decisions need good, systematic information about what is actually happening in schools so that they are informed but not blinded by the exceptional; reliable information about circumstances outside schools, and the ways in which they are changing; and access to the best available knowledge on what childen can do, given the chance. They need to be conscious of the material as well as the human changes required if modifications are to be brought about, and know that the funds and manpower will be forthcoming to support the changes. They need to think hard about the possible side effects of the actions they propose. They need to be aware that the goal they are pursuing is itself shifting; the task is to bring about an accommodation between what children can do, what schools and teachers can do, and what society offers and requires of its members. Each of the three has its own rhythm of change modified, to a greater or lesser degree, by changes in the other two.

In carrying out such a task it might be thought that the general educational viewpoint generated by primary school teachers would be particular useful. Unfortunately it seems extremely difficult to get anything like adequate representation of primary teachers or of primary school needs in national discussions. More than half the school children and about half the teachers in the country are lucky if a national committee includes two people with a main interest in primary education out of fifteen or more members, and even the two may not be involved in the day to day life of a school.

Teachers and Schools

Even so, the prime movers in developments in primary education have often been the teachers, and, of course, they have always been the ones to implement the innovations. During its final phase the Schools Council began to support groups of teachers undertaking experimental work. Its field officer team was always too small to keep in close touch with the work of more than a small proportion of classrooms, and the whole ethos, in the training system as well as, for the most part, in the Schools Council, was one of acting upon teachers rather than one of drawing out the gifts of some teachers and making them widely available. The process is not immediately attractive — to be creative oneself is so much more energizing — and requires a much more even-handed effort than has been common between the various groups active in the curriculum field and the teachers. It also requires fine judgement on all sides about what the whole state of teaching is, about what the priorities for the time being should be — to try to advance on many fronts at once is counterproductive — and how best to spread good practice.

Discipline and Development

It is curious how often developments in primary education suffer from the misconceptions of those outside who glance at the surface appearance of what is happening and assume that there is no underlying discipline or orderliness in the activities. For some the effect is sentimental pleasure in what is happening and for others a sense of disquiet that the 'real' world will come as too much of a shock to children who are supposedly allowed to do as they please. It is even worse when some inside primary education make the same mistake and then engage in practices that eschew forethought and fail to promote the inherent discipline required by the activities undertaken. The critics are right to ridicule that. Almost as bad is imitating an element in what is done well without developing the work to the point where the skills and ideas acquired provide a base for still further development. In art, for example, the work has too often been left at the stage of drawing and painting from close observation and the knowledge gained of form, texture, tone and colour — the vocabulary — has not been put to use in expressing feeling, in fantasy and imagination. The classroom display of children's work has too often become a matter of the overall attractiveness of its appearance, with every picture carefully mounted on two or three overlapping pieces of card, rather than a means of spreading ideas and information — which requires that the material is attractively presented so that it will be closely scrutinized, not so that it will simply provide an attractive backcloth. The example given earlier of misunderstanding the purpose of measuring by spans and paces is of the same kind.

These examples show something of the difficulties of

communication not only between HMI, LEA inspectors and advisers and teachers, but also between teachers. The main difficulties may come from misunderstandings about the functions of the details in the picture as a whole. No-one should begrudge time spent on making sure that the context as well as the example are understood, and the relationship between them is strong.

Notes

1. Blackie, J. (1982) p. 12, in The Open University, *Approaches to Evaluation*, E364, Block 2, Part 3, Milton Keynes, The Open University Press.
2. DES (1967) Plowden Report, paragraphs 635 and 638, London, HMSO.
3. Stone, A. L. (1949) *The Story of a School*, Ministry of Education, London, HMSO.
4. Hohmann, M., Banet, B. and Weikart, D. P. (1979) *Young Children in Action*, Ypsilanti, Michigan, The High/Scope Press.
5. Unstead, R. J. (1955) *Looking at History*, London, A. and C. Black.
6. House of Commons Education, Science and Arts Committee (1986) *Achievement in Primary Schools*, Third Report, Session 1985–86: HC 40–1, Volume 1, paragraph 10.46, London, HMSO.
7. ILEA (1985) *Improving Primary Schools*, paragraph 2.6, London, ILEA.
8. e.g. Froome, S. H. (1969) *The Mystique of Modern Maths*, in Cox, C. B. and Dyson, A. E. (Eds) *Black Paper 2*, London, The Critical Quarterly Society.
9. Plaskow, M. (Ed.) (1985) *Life and Death of the Schools Council*, p. 16, Lewes, The Falmer Press.
10. Wastnedge, E. R. (Ed.) (1967) *Nuffield Junior Science, Teachers' Guide*, London, Collins.
11. Matthews, G. (1967) *I do and I understand*, Edinburgh, Chambers.
12. First called Grant Related In-Service Training (GRIST).
13. Plaskow, M. (1985) *op. cit.*, p. 1.
14. Ennever, L. and Harlen, W. (1972) *With Objectives in Mind: Guide to Science 5–13*, London, MacDonald Educational.
15. Blyth, W. A. L., Cooper, K. R., Derricot, R., Elliott, G., Sumner, H.

and Waplington, A. (1976) *Place, Time and Society 8–13: Curriculum Planning in History, Geography and Social Science*, Glasgow and Bristol, Colins/ESL.

16. Cockerill, G. *The Middle Years*, p. 89, in Plaskow, M. (1985) *op. cit.*

Chapter 5

The Central Government's Role: 1964–1979

The Curriculum Study Group was especially concerned — as indicated by its encouragement of the Nuffield projects — with bringing the education system into line with modern requirements. Although it was replaced by the Schools Council, the central Government became increasingly interested in what schools were teaching, but publicly-expressed concerns about the service became more complex.

First, there continued to be the view, already referred to, that children of the day needed an education suited to the day and to what was yet to come, not to yesterday. Mathematics, science and technology would be increasingly important if Britain was to continue to earn its keep in the world. More attention had to be paid to the rest of the world and especially the mainland of Europe, hence the support for the teaching of a modern foreign language in primary schools, an experiment that broke down mainly on the practicalities of maintaining continuity of teaching in the primary schools over time and between primary and secondary schools as the children moved through; the difficulties were substantially those of providing teachers, even of French, with the skills and knowledge required in the numbers required.[1]

Organizational changes seemed to offer a way forward in education as in other aspects of life: secondary education should become comprehensive, the practice of streaming children in primary and secondary schools should be abandoned; higher education should be expanded; local government should be re-organized.

Secondly, there was criticism that children were learning less than they should in the old terms. Part of this impression no doubt came from the inclination of some members of each generation to believe that members of the next are showing signs of decline; a view that has persisted at least since the age of Socrates. Part also arose from the sense that the old system was changing and for the worse. Those in favour of changes in secondary schooling took the view that children should no longer be split between grammar schools and the rest at 11 because to do so was to be socially divisive, and — perhaps less significant among the advocates but more important to disappointed parents — because the process could not be carried out with justice in each case. That stance was opposed by those who saw the possible disappearance of grammar schools as a levelling down and leading to a loss of educational attainment by the brightest pupils. This distillation would no doubt be thought inadequate and maybe unjust by both sets of protagonists, but the trials and tribulations of secondary education are not the principal concern here.

What mattered from the primary school point of view was that the debate raised the question of the maintenance of standards in reading and arithmetic in primary schools, and to a lesser extent in history and geography because, it was thought, the schools would lack a steering mechanism when the 11-plus selection examination disappeared. The Plowden Report was seen as encouraging woolliness and hence a further lowering of standards of performance, so continuing the supposed decline generated by the Labour Government's Circular 10/65 which asked LEAs to prepare plans for the introduction of comprehensive secondary schools.

If the Plowden Report represented the optimistic view, then the Black Papers provided a medium and a focus for the pessimists. Both have their place in the continuing discussion if the bait can be taken without springing the trap. Bantock's warnings[2] about an over-reliance on 'discovery methods' should be taken very seriously. He is right to remind us that a knowledgeable guide and mentor is an invaluable companion if we are to learn as well as we might from the circumstances of our lives. If his warning encourages our mentors to put our heads into clamps so that our field of vision is restricted to no more than what they choose, then the warning does indeed turn into a trap.

The third public concern grew out of the first two. The education system, which had seemed to be more or less single minded, now showed little inner consistency, or so it was thought. If those in it differed in what they believed to be desirable, everyone could have a say, and everyone might justifiably worry.

In these circumstances it is hardly surprising that the Secretary of State, Margaret Thatcher, felt it right to set up a Committee of Inquiry, the Bullock Committee, to look into a specifically curriculum matter, the teaching of English. The trigger, as was acknowledged earlier, was the fall in the mean score of 11-year-olds in a national reading survey. The action was probably as significant as the formation of the Curriculum Study Group, perhaps more so, since it would have been possible to remit the enquiry to the Schools Council. Yet this time there was no serious outburst of opposition from either the teachers' associations or the LEAs.

The series of national surveys of the reading ability of 11- and 15-year-olds is discussed further in Chapter 7. The one held in 1970 is the most significant here. The mean scores of 11-year-olds fell by 0.81 to 14.19 on the Watts-Vernon Test and by 0.1 to 29.38 on the N.S.6 Test as compared with the immediately previous surveys in which they had been used. The Bullock Report[3] concluded that there had been no significant change in reading standards between 1960 and 1970 as shown by the NS6 test, but that 'the movement in Watts-Vernon scores from 1964 to 1970 just achieves significance (at the 5 per cent level), so that such movement as did occur was in all probability downwards.' There may have been a growing proportion of poor readers among children of unskilled and semi-skilled workers, and the national averages 'almost certainly' masked falling reading standards in areas with severe and educational problems. It is worth remembering that the children who formed the June, 1970,[4] sample would have entered infant classes some six or seven years previously, and junior classes in 1966. Their vital early years in learning to read could not possibly have been affected by either the Plowden Report or the effects of Circular 10/65. If there was a real decline in reading standards, and the report on the 1976/7 survey concludes[5] that there probably was not, then the reasons have to be sought elsewhere. Both faith and disbelief in the education system are influenced more by incident and the natural inclination of the observer than by conclusive, objective evidence, which is remarkably difficult to come by in any form that can be interpreted with confidence.

The 1972 White Paper: A Framework for Expansion

Provision for the Under-5s

Evidence for the effects of providing for the under-5s is particularly difficult to interpret. The arguments for making provision, or not, are social as well as educational. Are the children best off in their homes because that is where, according to the research of Barbara Tizard and others, they can get most adult attention and more chances of extending communication through language?[6] Or is it better if mothers can be freed of constant care of their young children so that they can lead fuller social lives and/or take up work earlier? Is the professional care provided in day nurseries and nursery classes and schools better for children and, taken together with the opportunities provided for movement and social play, do those advantages outweigh others that may come from longer periods spent in the home? To what extent is nursery education providing intellectual stimuli that will help children to make better progress when they transfer to infant classes? The answers are different for different children.

In broad policy terms, I believe that nursery education should be expanded as the 1972 White Paper proposed, but also linked much more closely to the Pre-school Playgroup and the Mother and Toddler provision, as well as to the Social Services care services for under-5s. This calls for much greater cooperation and coordination at central and local Government levels, and also enhanced relations between teachers, nursery nurses and parents. As was pointed out in Chapter 1, both the Plowden Committee in 1967 and the Government in the White Paper of 1972[7] proposed that nursery education should be available for all 3- and 4-year-olds whose parents wished them to have it, and assumed that that would amount to 50 per cent of 3-year-olds and 90 per cent of 4-year-olds. The White Paper envisaged an expansion of provision taking a decade, with priority in the early stages going to LEAs 'with substantial areas of social deprivation, urban and rural'. The White Paper also reminded its readers of the contribution that parents and playgroups could make. The hoped-for expansion was truncated by the financial effects of the oil crisis in 1973/4.

Thus, although the 1988 Select Committee Report on the education of under-5s[8] was able to record a steady expansion of places for the under-5s since 1973, it also pointed out that the 1972 White Paper's aim had not been achieved. Generally, nursery and other maintained provision for under-5s is more common in deprived areas and in urban areas and less so in more affluent and rural areas. Independent provision, mainly in playgroups, is greatest where maintained provision is least. In 1987 there were almost as many under-5s in infant classes as in nursery schools or classes: 21 per cent as against 23 per cent. The former included few 3-year-olds. It is difficult to estimate the total percentage of under-5s being cared for/educated outside their homes because some information relates to the number of places available, which may be occupied by different children at different times of the day or week; and because some children use more than one kind of provision, for example they may be cared for by childminders and attend a nursery class or playgroup for part of the day. The fact that some providers take children from a few weeks old and others not until 3 or 4 adds to the difficulty of interpreting statistics. However, the following, taken from Table 1 in the Select Committee's Report, give some idea of the relative weights of the forms of provision in 1986:

Childminders	127	Local Authority day nurseries	29
Private day nurseries	25	Nursery classes/schools	267
Playgroups	409	Independent schools	32
		Primary schools (i.e. infant classes)	246

(Numbers given in thousands)

The total population of 0–4-year-olds was 2.97 million, including 1.19 million 3- and 4-year-olds.

The result is that children entering junior schools may have been cared for wholly by their parents before coming to school at 5. They may have been looked after by childminders, registered or casual; have attended a day nursery for nearly five years; they may have had one year or two years in a voluntary playgroup concentrating on social development; they may have had one or two years in a nursery class or school which concerned itself also with intellectual development; they may have had two years or three years of infant education; or a mixture of these plus experience of some other forms of provision, such as being looked after by a relative or neighbour, or a period in hospital.

Improvements in Statutory and Higher Education

The 1972 White Paper confirmed the Government's determination to see the replacement of outdated school buildings, most of which were primary schools. It expressed the hope — control, as of so much else, was in the hands of the LEAs — that non-teaching costs in schools would continue to increase, overall, at 3 per cent per annum on average. It proposed that there should be an improvement of 10 per cent in 'staffing standards' to provide a national pupil:teacher ratio of 18.5:1 by 1981 for primary and secondary schools taken together. In addition, 25,000 teachers were presumed to be necessary for the expansion of nursery education. Plans were announced for changes in higher education, including teacher training, as was the intention to form an Advisory Committee on the Supply and Training of Teachers, to become better known as ACSET, 'Training' being replaced by 'Education'. Its third paragraph points out that the White Paper is concerned with 'matters of scale, organization and cost rather than educational content'. As Edward Simpson has pointed out,[9] the use of the word 'framework' in the title was not accidental, and reflected a relationship between the central Government and others, including LEAs. At its best, the relationship was one in which the Government brought together and expressed commonly held objectives.

The White Paper itself warned that its projections might be overtaken by outside events, for example 'the recent signs of a falling birth-rate'.[10] Even within a few weeks of the publication of the White Paper, the Prime Minister, Edward Heath, told the January, 1973, Conference of the Society of Education Officers that too much attention was being given to finance and organization and reminded his audience that most people are concerned with what is taught in schools than with the ways in which they are organized.[11] Neither the writers of the White Paper nor anyone else anticipated the changes that would flow from the oil crisis.

The fall in the birth rate in the United Kingdom began when the Plowden Committee was still sitting. In 1964 over a million babies were born. In 1977 the number had fallen to about 650,000. The number has increased since then, reaching about 750,000 in 1980 and, after small falls, much the same in 1985 and 1986.[12] The number of children over 5 years of age in maintained primary schools in England fell from 4,763,000[13] in 1975 to 3,644,962 in 1985,[14] a fall of more than 23 per cent. The possibility of a fall had been no more than a small cloud on the horizon of the Plowden Report: a footnote on page 126 referred to an expectation that by the mid-1970s the average annual age group would be 880,000 unless 'the most recent trends in births continue [when] some downward movement is likely'.[15]

Profound financial and attitudinal changes arose from the reducing number of children to be educated and the effects of the oil crisis. They were heightened by the other main demographic change: the increase, current and prospective, in the number of people over 65 who would make calls on the social services' budgets. Suddenly the education service was having to put a much better argued case for its funding.

The Assessment of Performance Unit

No change of government could alter these underlying factors. The expansion of nursery education largely came to an end, and anxieties about the direction and quality of the education service continued. The formation of the Assessment of Performance Unit (APU) in the DES was announced in 1974[16] and it was finally established in 1975. Its terms of reference were:

> To promote the development of methods of assessing and monitoring the achievement of children at school, and to seek to identify the incidence of under-achievement.[17]

The work of the APU was subject to the scrutiny of a Consultative Committee, under an independent chairman, eighteen of the members being nominated by LEAs and teachers' associations and the other 12 directly appointed by the Secretary of State. The APU formulated a view of the curriculum for assessment purposes which was intended to cut across timetable boundaries: when looking at language, for example, it would be concerned with the development of language generated by the study of science, mathematics, art and the rest, and similarly with science and mathematics. It was intended that it should also be concerned with physical development, aesthetic development, personal and social development. Language would in the end include English and foreign languages.

The establishment of the Unit was treated with some suspicion, as Denis Lawton[18] says, because it was seen as a means of monitoring standards; because teachers might teach to the tests, it would exercise some control over the curriculum; and it would encourage LEAs to indulge in even less desirable testing of their own. In fact, as Lawton agrees, the APU did not become an accountabilty monster. Its work was designed to provide information which others could use when forming views on what should be done. As the APU memorandum says, the survey reports 'provide sources of information for those concerned which curriculum development' and the short reports for teachers do not attempt to tell them 'what they should do, or how they should teach in the light of the findings, but they do suggest questions and patterns which teachers might wish to bear in mind when considering their own classroom practice'.[19] The APU reports are complex, for they deal with complex material, but they are certainly not obscure and they contain much information that ought to be used avidly by the teaching profession. Sadly, it has not been so, and one wonders what should be done to enable teachers to be better informed. Other professionals also have their fashionable complaints and cures with slipped discs, tonsillectomies or Valium, but they, like teaching, require a more laborious attention to fine detail in their day-to-day practice than the sweep of fashion excites.

In the event the exploratory work on aesthetics and personal and social development did not come to fruition. The APU has commissioned programmes on English, including reading, writing, speaking and listening, and on mathematics and science for 11-year-olds, i.e. at the end of the traditional primary school stage. The surveys are of about 2 per cent of the age group. The surveys are essentially national surveys. In order to cover a wide range of understanding and skills without making the test onerous, no single child is presented with the whole of the mathematics material used. The sample is too small in any one LEA for conclusions to be drawn about the LEA as a whole. The surveys include pencil and paper tests and also practical tests where appropriate. These stimulate carefully arranged conversation between the child and the tester. The experience gained has opened up new possibilities in the standardized assessment of children's skills and knowledge and there is little doubt that the experience gained will be important in the arrangements made for the assessment of children's performance in the National Curriculum.

The Great Debate

The launch of the APU was an element in the growing activity of the central Government. It was by no means all. In the early autumn of 1976 there were widespread reports of a memorandum, the so-called Yellow Book, that the Secretary of State, Shirley Williams, had sent to the Prime Minister, James (now Lord) Callaghan. So far as primary schools were concerned, the opinion was expressed that more account was being taken of individual differences between children and that this 'child-centred' approach could greatly advance learning for a large number of them. But it required teaching of high quality, with careful planning and a clear understanding of aims. This was becoming better understood, as was the need to recognize the different capabilities of individual teachers. The need was to restore rigour without damaging the real benefits of child-centred developments. Parents did not always recognize the advantages of the child-centred approach, even when it was well applied. The time, it was argued, was almost certainly ripe for a corrective shift of emphasis.

In his comments[20] on the document in a letter to the Prime Minister, the then Chairman of the Schools Council, Sir Alex Smith, complained about the unconditional praise given to HMI, the lack of self-criticism of the DES — both of which had official positions in the Schools Council — while teachers and the Schools Council were criticized for failures of the education system. He was 'not very disturbed by the suggestion . . . that there is need for a core curriculum'.

The Prime Minister had set out his views on the education service in a speech given at Ruskin College, Oxford, on the 18th October, 1976. He

> commented on the enthusiasm and dedication of the teaching profession, but suggested that the increasing complexity of modern life meant that standards in many areas, including education, needed to go on rising. There was, he felt, a widespread feeling that this was not happening, and it would be to the advantage of all involved in education if these concerns were aired, ill-founded fears put to rest, and shortcomings remedied.[21]

The 'Great Debate' on education that followed in February and March, 1977, was promoted by the Secretary of State, Shirley Williams. The four subjects it addressed at a series of regional conferences were: The School Curriculum 5–16; The Assessment of Standards; The Education and Training of Teachers; and School and Working Life. It would be difficult to identify any later events as being shaped by the ensuing debate; it was part of the weft contributing to the cloth rather than being a determinant of the pattern. The pattern was one of increasing political and public interest in the education service and concern about its effectiveness in modern social conditions. The subject was on the agendas of all political parties.

It is worth noticing that the accompanying DES document[22] referred to the curriculum of the whole of the Statutory age range 5–16, an age span that was to be carried right through to the National Curriculum. Worries were expressed that the differences between the programmes and achievements of primary schools (and secondary schools, of course, but they are not the focus here) produced inequalities of opportunity; made continuity between primary and secondary schools more difficult; and caused difficulties as children moved about the country with their parents. Although the thrust was mainly directed at secondary schools, it was also noted that the primary schools paid too little attention to the fact that children were growing up in an industrial society.

A distinction was made between a common curriculum and a common core. Differences of opinion were noted as to whether a common core would be 'a basic minimum of information and skills' to be acquired by all, or whether it covered English and mathematics, and if it did, what was to be included under those, or indeed any other, subject headings. One example of divergence given concerned the teaching of science, which in one primary school might lead to observation and experiment and in another be confined to gleaning information from books.

The DES eased itself through the crumbling garden wall. The regional conferences were followed by the publication of a Green Paper,[23] which rehearsed the subjects discussed in the 'Great Debate' and reminded its readers that:

> It would not be compatible with the duty of the Secretaries of State to 'promote the education of the people of England and Wales', or with their accountability to Parliament, to abdicate from leadership on educational issues which have become a matter of lively public concern. The Secretaries of State will therefore seek to establish a broad agreement with their partners in the education

service on a framework for the curriculum, and, particularly, on whether, because there are aims common to all schools and to all pupils at certain stages, there should be a 'core' or 'protected part'.[24]

The Contraction of the Education Service

The Green Paper referred to 1977 as being a watershed year. Until then there had been a great expansion of education and of the number of teachers — about 50 per cent more between 1966 and 1976;[25] the increase resulted in there being a large proportion of inexperienced teachers and high mobility. The 'planned contraction of the training capacity' for teachers would reduce the number of new teachers each year from 40,000 at its peak to 'fewer than 20,000' each year by the early 1980s. There should 'as soon as possible' be a wholly graduate entry to the teaching profession. It is interesting to notice, in view of later decisions, that there were worries that intending teachers might not have 'a sufficient command of the English language' or be sufficiently numerate; that the courses might not pay enough attention to the world outside education and to the multi-cultural nature of society; whether enough was being done to equip students with the 'essential intellectual mastery' of the subjects they would teach; whether they were sufficiently trained to direct children's work and ensure good discipline; and what the effects would be of increasing the integration of teacher training and higher education. It envisaged a fourfold expansion of teachers — counted as full-time equivalents — on in-service training, including support during their probationary year. It expressed support for the idea that in-service training should be based 'on specific objectives and problems of individual schools and . . . therefore [be] to that extent school-based'. It also announced the channelling of funds through the Manpower Services Commission for in-service training, and foresaw, 'in the longer term', the possibility of specific grants for in-service training. There was an expectation that parents would be brought more into the management of schools following the soon to be published Taylor Report.[26]

It was acknowledged that there had been cuts in public expenditure on education amounting to £150 millions (2.4 per cent) in the previous two years; that constraint was still necessary though a modest rate of growth should be possible by the end of the decade; but that it should be remembered that there had been a great increase in public spending on education between 1965 and 1975. The January 1975 White Paper revealed a significant change of perception by the Central Government, the significance of which has become more apparent with the passing years. A block grant for local authorities had replaced specific grants for education in 1958 but until 1975, the

> expenditure by local authorities was everywhere subsumed within the respective expenditure totals for the services to which they contributed; the total of planned spending by local authorities was nowhere even added up.[27]

Subsequent to 1975, the combination of the economic crisis and record increases in local authority spending led the Government to consider local authority spending as a whole. The result was that the 'spending' Departments, including the DES, were in a weaker position in proposing particular policies to LEAs. Locally, the movement towards corporate management in local authorities also shifted concern towards the totality of expenditure and so pressed education committees and their officers even more to be sure that any case they put forward for increased expenditure, or even for maintaining expenditure, was convincing.

The Green Paper added to the sense of there being a watershed by taking the central Government to the point of discussing publicly how the teaching force should be managed, particularly as it contracted in parallel with, though a step behind, the fall in the number of pupils.

DES Interest in LEA Curricular Policies

It presaged the issue of what was to be DES Circular 14/77 asking

LEAs to let it know what their curricular policies and practices were. It was expected that teachers would be brought into the discussion when replies were being formulated, but the focus of the enquiry was on LEA policies, not on the policies or practices of individual schools. All but one LEA replied, though not all replies were judged to be satisfactory by those reporting the findings, which were published in 1979.[28] The idea was again broached of an agreed framework for the curriculum as a means of improving 'the consistency and quality of school education across the country . . . HM Inspectorate was asked to formulate a view of the curriculum on the basis of its knowledge of schools.'

Notes

1. Burstall, C., Jamieson, M., Cohen, S. and Hargreaves, M. (1974) *Primary French in the Balance*, Slough, NFER.
2. Bantock, G. H. (1969) *Discovery Methods*, in Cox, C. B. and Dyson, A. E. (Eds) *Black Paper 2*, London, The Critical Quarterly Society.
3. DES (1975) Bullock Report, paragraph 2.29, London, HMSO.
4. Start, K. B. and Wells, B. K. (1972) *The Trend of Reading Standards*, Slough, NFER.
5. DES/HMI (1978) *Primary Education in England*, p. 162, London, HMSO.
6. Tizard, B. and Hughes, M. (1984) *Young children learning, talking and thinking at home and at school*, London, Fontana.
7. DES Cmnd. 5174 (1972) *Education: A Framework for Expansion*, London, HMSO — see also page 10.
8. House of Commons Education, Science and Arts Committee (1989) *Educational Provision for the Under Fives*, First Report, Volume 1, Session 1988–89, 30–I, London, HMSO.
9. Simpson, E. (1986) p. 22, in Ranson, S. and Tomlinson, J. (Eds) *The Changing Government of Education*, London, Allen and Unwin.
10. DES Cmnd. 5174, *op. cit.*
11. Simpson, E. (1986) p. 23, *op. cit.*
12. Statham, J., Mackinnon, D. and Cathcart, H., (1989) *The Education Factfile*, figure 2.4, p. 9, London, Hodder and Stoughton.
13. DES/WO (1977) *A Study of School Building*, p. 49, London, HMSO.

14. DES (1986) *Educational Statistical Bulletin 6/86*: the figure is the full-time equivalent pupils' number. Neither of the figures includes children of primary school age in schools deemed to be secondary schools.
15. DES (1967) Plowden Report, London, HMSO.
16. DES (1975) Cmnd. 5720.
17. DES/APU (1985) Memorandum submitted to the House of Commons Education, Science and Arts Committee, see *Achievement in Primary Schools*, Minutes of Evidence, Session 1984–85, HC 48, p. 320, London, HMSO.
18. Lawton, D. (1986) *Curriculum and Assessment*, in Ranson, S. and Tomlinson, J. (Eds) *The Changing Government of Education*, *op. cit.*
19. DES/APU (1985) memorandum, p. 321, *op. cit.*
20. Smith, Sir A. (1985) p. 107, in Plaskow, M. (Ed.), *Life and Death of the Schools Council*, Lewes, Falmer Press.
21. DES (1977) *Educating Our Children, Four Subjects for Debate*, London, DES.
22. *ibid*.
23. DES Cmnd. 6869 (1977) *Education in Schools, A Consultative Document*, London, HMSO.
24. *ibid.*, p. 12.
25. *ibid.*, p. 24.
26. DES (1977) *A New Partnership of Our Schools*, Committee of Inquiry chaired by Thomas Taylor, London, HMSO.
27. Simpson, E., (1986) p. 25ff., in Ranson, S. and Tomlinson, J. (Eds) *The Changing Government of Education*, *op. cit.* provides a fuller discussion of this issue.
28. DES (1979) *Local Authority Arrangements for the School Curriculum*, London, HMSO.

Chapter 6

Interventions of the Central Government and Parliament: 1979–1989

By the time the discussion of the results was underway, the 1979 general election had taken place, a Conservative government was in office with Margaret Thatcher as Prime Minister, and Mark Carlisle was the Secretary of State for Education. The change certainly did not delay the progress of the debate.

HMI and DES Views of the Curriculum

HM Inspectorate's *A View of the Curriculum*[1] was published in 1980. Its foreword makes it clear that it is based on recent surveys and inspections, including the national survey of primary education.[2] It stresses that the document is a contribution to the national discussion, and hopes that it will reach a wider than professional readership. The section on primary education argued for the continued recognition of differences between pupils, whatever their causes, and for a broad curriculum. Children should be engaged in a programme that allows them to work in a variety of social relationships, extends their powers of language, and generally increases the range of their experiences. In mathematics priority should be given to acquiring skill in using whole numbers up to 100, but nearly everyone should go far beyond that. Two appendices suggested in broad terms for reading and in rather more detail for mathematics, what children could be expected to learn in primary schools. Topics chosen for study should allow for the characteristics of the children, the knowledge of the teachers and the availability of resources. What is included should be instrinsically worthwhile and repeated only deliberately and to extend learning. Observational skills should be nurtured so that children have information upon which their imaginations can work and be expressed through painting, modelling, movement, music and storytelling. The teaching of science should be further developed. Children should acquire a sense of history and of geographical influences, both of which should contribute to an understanding of today's multicultural society, as should the study of Christianity and other major world faiths. A foreign language should only be taught where conditions are favourable. It concluded that whatever was to be decided nationally, much must be left to LEAs and schools to settle so as to allow for differences between schools and between children; and no decisions could be taken once and for all, for times change.

Within a few days, the DES had published its next contribution, a consultative document entitled *Towards a Framework for the School Curriculum*.[3] It referred back to the HMI document. It proposed that English, mathematics, science and physical education should be included in the programmes for all children of school age, in addition to Religious Education for which provision must already be made under the law. The first two should each be taught for at least 10 per cent of school time, a proposal that came in for critical comment from the primary school side because there were and are probably no schools that spend so little time on these two aspects of their work, even when work in the subjects was narrowly defined. When the consultations were over, a new document was prepared and published in March 1981 under the title *The School Curriculum*.[4] It asserted that:

> curriculum policies should be developed and implemented on the basis of the existing statutory relationship between the partners.

(i.e. teachers and LEAs); that local authorities had

> a responsibility to formulate curricular policies and objectives which meet national policies and objectives,

command local assent, and can be applied by each school
to its own circumstances.

Neither the Government nor the local authorities should
specify in detail what the schools should teach.

DES Action on Science and Foreign Languages

The Secretaries of State decided that the DES and Welsh Office
(rather than teachers, LEAs or Schools Council) would take on the
next stage in deciding the development of the teaching of science
and foreign languages. The document recognized the limitations of
describing the curriculum in subject terms, but did so on the grounds
that secondary school timetables were almost always devised in them,
and because parents and employers would be familiar with them.
However, no percentages of time were proposed this time. Attention
was again drawn to the multicultural nature of society today; to the
effects of technological change; to the importance of ensuring that
equal curricular opportunity is available to boys and girls. Curricular
breadth was considered important, as were personal and social
development. Continuity should be established between primary
and secondary schools. In the former, high priority was and should
be attached to English and mathematics, but set in a broad context.
Three aspects of primary schools' programmes picked out for
comment were: *topic work*, where it was important to establish a
clear overall plan and progression, and to link the work with reading,
writing and mathematics; *science*, about which the Secretaries of
State intended to do more; *art and craft*, in which direct observation
should be encouraged, and there should be more three dimensional
work, some of which might provide an introduction to technology;
and *French*, where, once more, it was urged that the subject should
be included only if continuity could be secured as children moved
through to secondary schools.

Paragraph 62, out of 64, warned that the Secretaries of State
would wish to inform themselves later about the action taken by local
authorities in the light of the paper and within the resources available

to them. DES Circular 6/81 asked LEAs to review their curricular policies and the ways in which they were made known; to consider the extent to which the provision in maintained schools was consistent with that policy; and to plan future developments within the resources available. Two years later, with Sir Keith Joseph well established as Secretary of State for Education, DES Circular 8/83 asked the authorities to report what they and their schools had done as a result of their reviews. The responses were summarized and commented upon in *Local Authority Policies for the School Curriculum*.[5] By then, two other seminal documents had been produced by the DES: *Teaching Quality*,[6] which began the process of establishing new criteria that teacher training courses would have to meet; and *Better Schools*.[7]

Teaching Quality

Teaching Quality opened up the discussion about criteria that should be met in the initial training of teachers. It argued that all primary school teachers should take a particular responsibility for one aspect of the curriculum, act as a consultant for colleagues and where appropriate teach the subject to other classes than their own (paragraph 33). The last five words imply that the role of class teacher was still to be paramount. It reminded readers that all entering teaching from September 1984 would have to be able to show that they had reached certain minimum levels in English and mathematics (science has now been added) (paragraph 54). Courses should include at least two full years devoted to subject studies which, for intending primary school teachers, might cover a wide area of the curriculum; methodology should be taught so as to relate it to the ages of the children in view and should always include methods of teaching English and mathematics for intending primary school teachers; there should be practical experience of teaching involving practising teachers (paragraph 64). Students should not be awarded a Bachelor of Education degree or a Post Graduate Certificate of Education unless their practical classroom work was satisfactory (paragraph 68). The formal assessment of teacher performance was considered to be necessary and should be based on classroom visits by the headteacher or head of department, an appraisal of the children's work and of the contribution the teacher makes to school life generally (paragraph 92). Distinction was made between the validation of teacher training courses, which is concerned with academic standards, and the approval of courses, which is concerned with the suitability of the courses as preparations for school teaching. The latter is concerned with the 'broad framework and structure' of the courses and the former with their detailed content.

The Paper recognized the increasingly complex task that teachers had to undertake and proposed greater differentiation in training while maintaining a unified, primary/secondary teaching profession. Pupil:teacher ratios had become more generous as the number of pupils in primary schools fell. In the view of the writers, this meant that now 'it should be possible . . . to deploy teachers more effectively and hence to maintain staffing standards even with a slight tightening of the pupil teacher ratio.' As numbers of pupils now began to fall in secondary schools, 'it will be desirable to moderate the reduction in the number of teachers in secondary schools . . . *if advantage is taken of the scope for more effective use of teachers in primary schools* (my italics)'.[8] This was necessary so that the secondary schools, now smaller on average, could maintain a broad *and well-taught* curriculum (paragraph 21). Yet paragraph 31, while recognizing the advantages that come from each primary school class being the responsibility of one teacher, made the point strongly that:

> teachers [in primary schools] are rarely able to deal satisfactorily with all aspects of the curriculum from their own knowledge. In some cases help from a member of staff with specialist expertise may be sufficient; in others, especially with older children, it is desirable for classes or other groups of children to be taught for particular topics by teachers with specialist expertise.

HMI were quoted[9] as finding it 'disturbing that, in nearly a quarter of the primary school lessons seen, teachers showed signs of insecurity in the subject being taught. This is a far higher proportion than in the secondary schools in the sample . . . '

Paragraph 33 argues that all primary school teachers should be equipped to take 'a particular responsibility for one aspect of the curriculum (such as science, mathematics or music), to act as consultants to their colleagues on that aspect and, where appropriate, to teach it to classes other than their own.'

Table 2 of the document showed that in January 1982 the national disparity between primary school and secondary school staffing was:

	PTR*	Average size of class (estimated)
Primary schools	22.5	25.4
Secondary schools	16.6	21.3

* The ratios of the numbers of pupils to the numbers of qualified teachers actually employed in the (maintained) schools.

Whenever one sees such figures it is important to remember that primary schools vary in size proportionately much more than secondary schools do, and that larger primary schools pay for the necessarily more generous staffing of small primary schools. For most primary school children the figures are less generous than they seem from such tables. Even without that, I can think of no justification, then or now, for proposing that the staffing standards of secondary schools should be improved at the expense of primary school children, especially given the paper's own argument for increased flexibility in staffing primary schools.

Better Schools

Better Schools addressed itself to the dual issues of improving the quality of the education service and getting the most from the resources put into it. It says there is much to admire in what schools do, but some are failing seriously and even the best do not always set themselves objectives 'well matched with the demands of modern life' (paragraph 2). Nevertheless, it was recognized that primary schools generally offer, to a greater extent than in the 1950s, a broad curriculum, teach English and mathematics in ways that transcend simple skills, teach science, art and craft as an integral part of the curriculum, introduce history and geography effectively in topic and project work, encourage pupils to learn by active participation, use computers on a wide scale (paragraph 5). Personal and social development is fostered systematically (paragraph 7). But standards should be better, and enterprise and adaptability be promoted (paragraph 9).

So far as primary and middle schools are concerned, about three-quarters were judged to be weak in curriculum planning and its implementation. About three-quarters of the schools had curricular guidelines for English and mathematics but even in these they often did not make explicit the progression being sought and there were 'rarely effective mechanisms for ensuring that declared curricular policies were reflected in the day-to-day work of most teachers and pupils.' The best practice of an individual teacher is emulated throughout only a minority of schools (paragraph 17). In paragraphs 18 and following:

> The mistaken belief, once widely held, that a concentration on basic skills is by itself enough to improve achievements in literacy and numeracy has left its mark: many children are still given too little opportunity for work in the scientific, practical and aesthetic areas of the curriculum which increases not only their understanding within these areas but also their literacy and numeracy. In a majority of schools over-concentration on the practice of basic skills in literacy and numeracy unrelated to a context in which they are needed means that those skills are insufficiently extended and applied.

In about half of the classes, it was said, there was too little oral discussion and practical problem solving and too much direction by teachers. Judgements about children were too often underestimates because too much attention was paid to a child's background. Unfortunately the children and their parents too often accepted the resultant underexpectations. There was a need for children to be more rigorous and persevering. The results of assessment and testing should be used much more to ensure 'progress and continuity' of learning.

In paragraph 22 the point was again stressed that more use should be made of subject consultants and it was regretted that even where they were appointed:

> it is unusual for them to be given time, the status and encouragement to enable them to prepare and offer support to their colleagues and to exert the necessary influence on the whole curriculum of the school.

Reference was made to Sir Keith Joseph's 1984 speech to the North of England Conference and to the 'widespread acceptance' of his expression of the need to improve standards achieved by pupils and to the need to develop a 'broad agreement about the objectives and content of the school curriculum'. The advantages of the latter were seen to be that there would be a clearer view on what schools should be achieving and, consequently, they could be more fairly judged; parents, employers and the public would have a better idea of what support they should be giving; it would be possible to raise teachers' expectations and pupils' achievements generally and to remove preconceptions based on sex or ethnic origin; although there would continue to be differences from school to school, none should fall below an acceptable level. It would take some years to achieve an initial agreement, and whatever was decided would have to be modified from time to time. A recently issued policy statement on the teaching of science[10] was thought to represent the means through which agreed curricular statements would be made known. They would then be interpreted at three levels. At national level the curricular policy would inform the Secretaries of State when accounting to Parliament and in their statutory duties of promoting 'education . . . and the progressive development of institutions devoted to that purpose', in securing that local authorities execute their educational duties effectively, and in derivative functions, for example those concerned with the supply and training of teachers. At the LEA level, the curricular policy would provide a framework for making decisions relating to a wide range of provision for schools, the deployment of teachers and advisers. At school level, it would affect the organization and delivery of what is offered to pupils. The operation of the policies would not mean national uniformity, 'diversity is healthy'. Any statutory arrangements should facilitate the satisfactory resolution of conflicts as they occur (paragraphs 30–37).

LEAs were given credit for having formulated curricular policies over the previous three years. Most schools had set out their aims in writing and many LEAs had arrangements for discovering whether LEA and school aims were compatible; a number had schemes for schools' self-evaluation; and staffing and advisory staff policies were being affected to the point, in some cases, of there being curricular-led staffing policies [unfortunately, nearly always for secondary schools, not primary, NT]. Although the need for breadth, balance and relevance was recognized, there were few examples where the translation into practice of the last was made clear. Comparatively few LEAs had translated curricular policies into teaching approaches and methods; had considered continuity between primary and secondary schools; had given enough attention to differentiation according to individual pupils' needs; had thought, especially with regard to secondary schools, about elements of the curriculum not taught as separate subjects [a welcome abandonment here of the term 'cross-curricular', NT]; had paid enough attention to the role of employers in curricular development. Verdict: a good start but more to do (paragraphs 39–42).

The lists of the purposes of learning were quoted in Chapter 2. The principles of breadth, balance, differentiation and relevance were regarded as being 'at the heart of successful classroom practice in the primary phase'. 'The fact that their application is . . . usually expressed [in the document] in relation to subjects should not be misinterpreted . . . Such a description implies no particular view of timetabling or teaching approach. Nor does it deny that learning involves the mastery of processes as well as the acquisition of knowledge, skills and understanding' (paragraph 52). After discussion about the Government's long term intention to bring 80–90 per cent of all 16-year-olds at least to the level of achievement now expected of and achieved by average pupils, and the implications of that for defining levels of achievement, *Better Schools* goes on to identify three immediate tasks for the Government: to publish an account of LEA responses to Circular 3/83 — which it did;[11] to enter into consultations on national statements about individual subjects; to publish a further statement in relation to the organization and content of the 5–16 curriculum (paragraph 88).

Paragraph 212 expressed the view that what needed to be done could be managed, in the main, within the existing legal framework which 'gives freedom to each LEA to maintain its existing pattern of school organization and, if it wishes, to propose changes in that pattern'. Changes would be required to harness the energies of parents and others in a reformed system of school government, and they were established through the Education (No. 2) Act, 1986.

The House of Commons Select Committee

The House of Commons Education, Science and Arts Committee is an all-Party, backbenchers' committee which keeps a check on the work of the DES on behalf of the House of Commons. It began an extended look at primary education in June 1984 which resulted in its report published in the autumn of 1986, *Achievement in Primary Schools*.[12] It considered a number of aspects of primary education and notably the curriculum With relatively minor reservations, it commended the view of the curriculum taken in *Better Schools* and in the HMI series, *Matters for Discussion*, and in available LEA documents. The Committee pointed out that *Science 5–16: A statement of policy*[13] had many advantages as a definition of an aspect of the curriculum. It drew on existing material, including APU findings of what children can do; it recognized the need for the detailed choice of material to be related to the natures and circumstances of the children actually being taught; it recognized the need for progression and continuity and for the work to be in tune with what is done in other parts of the curriculum; it advocated a practical approach; it pointed up the role of LEA advisory services and teacher trainers. The Select Committee thought that similar statements should be produced on other aspects of the curriculum, (paragraph 7.15).

It went further than *Better Schools* and proposed that there should be a change in the law requiring the Secretaries of State to produce such statements, and that LEAs and governors of county, controlled and special schools should be required to consider the Secretary of State's curricular policy in the process of determining the curricular policy of the LEA or school. 'All LEAs should be required to show, within a time limit, how they are supporting schools in providing the declared curricular range for children between 3 and 16 and, if they choose, what they are promoting in addition.' Governors should arrange for the production of schemes of work showing how the curriculum is covered and lodge copies and subsequent amendments with the LEA and HMI (paragraph 7.8).

The Committee considered that the arrangements proposed would avoid the Secretary of State getting into the position of defining the detail of what was taught and hoped that assurances given by the Secretary of State on this would be kept then and by future Secretaries of State. The proposals would not require a Secretary of State to get into 'the more difficult issues of levels of children's performance'. Nor would they, nor should they, require a definition of methods of teaching or school organization (paragraph 7.9). The changes would considerably increase the weight of the Secretary of State's pronouncements on the curriculum. The presumption was that the statements should represent a broad consensus, and it was important that the discussion leading to the statements should be public. To that end, a new Consultative Committee should be set up 'semi-detached from the DES and representing views from within and outside the education service'. Its function should be to advise the Secretary of State on the curriculum. The Consultative Committee should be supported by teams consisting mainly of primary and secondary school teachers, LEA advisers and HMI whose job would be to prepare papers for the

Committee on aspects of the curriculum. There might need to be an intermediate group, drawn from the support groups, to advise the Committee on the relationships between the aspects of the curriculum so that a holistic view was also available based, for example, on the analysis used by HMI in *Curriculum Matters 2*[14] (paragraphs 7.11 to 7.13). The report was accepted unanimously by the Conservative and Labour Party members of the Committee.

The Final Step: A National Curriculum

It is small wonder that after a due interval, the Secretary of State, by now Kenneth Baker, should make his announcement to the Select Committee that he intended to propose to Parliament that it should enact a National Curriculum. The first substantial and written account of what might be proposed was published in July, 1987, under the title, *The National Curriculum 5-16, a consultation document.*[15] The consultation period was intended to last until 30th September, and although in the end the period — crossing the summer holidays — was extended, many complained that they had insufficient time to respond adequately. About 10,000 replies containing millions of words were submitted in response by the end of the year. Perhaps the officials given the job of reading them remembered Blaise Pascal's regret that he hadn't time to write briefly. Julian Haviland,[16] taking on the independent responsibility for sieving the replies, reported that 'the principle was overwhelmingly approved: [he could not] recall one response, however, that endorsed without reservation the structure of the curriculum which the Government was proposing.'

In fact, the structure survived the handiwork of the Parliamentary draughtsman and Parliament itself with little change into the Education Reform Act, 1988, though with some debating excursions about how much of the curriculum would be National Curriculum and how much not. The brief account here is partly to allow continuity in the story and partly to pick up a few points that still seem to be causing confusion or uncertainty. References will be given only where they are important in supporting a particular point of view. In any particular case, reference should be made to the Act[17] itself and, as with all other Acts of Parliament, it has to be remembered that the interpretation of what is said is ultimately for the Courts.

Religious Education

Religious education is not part of the National Curriculum but its provision is still a legal requirement for schools. All pupils in attendance at a maintained school (Section 6(1)), shall attend an act of collective worship each day, except that children may be excused from attending acts of collective worship or religious education, or both (Section 9(3)) either wholly or partly. The act of worship need no longer be at the beginning of the school day, nor must it be for all eligible children together. The act of worship shall be wholly or mainly of a broadly Christian character (Section 7(1)), at least taking a school term as a whole. However, a headteacher may, after consulting the school's governing body, consider that the backgrounds of the pupils make it unsuitable that the acts of worship shall be 'broadly Christian' and apply to the local Standing Advisory Council on Religious Education (SACRE) for exemption. That Council, which has to be constituted by the LEA, must decide whether to agree to the headteacher's request and give its decision in writing. Religious education will continue to be subject to an agreed syllabus as formerly, and that syllabus 'shall reflect the fact that the religious traditions in Great Britain are in the main Christian whilst taking account of the teaching and practices of the other principle religions represented in Great Britain' (Section 8(3)). If a school cannot provide the form of religious education required by a child who has been withdrawn from its own provision, and he or she cannot conveniently be sent to another maintained school that can provide what is required, then the child may be withdrawn from the school 'during such periods of time as are reasonable' to receive religious education elsewhere than in a maintained school (Section 9(4)). Such withdrawal must take place at the beginning or end of a school session (Section 9(6)), and the LEA must be satisfied that the arrangements made are satisfactory in the case of pupils at county or voluntary schools; in the case of a grant-maintained school it is the governing body that must be content.

Key Stages and the Foundation Subjects

The Secretary of State has the duty of establishing the National Curriculum as soon as is reasonably practicable — in effect from September 1989 with gradually increasing definition — and of revising it as he considers necessary. The definition is settled through the issue of Statutory Orders about each foundation subject specifying:

(a) attainment targets
(b) programmes of study, and
(c) assessment arrangements

It is very important to notice that an Order made in this connection may not specify the amount of time that should be allocated to the teaching of a programme of study or any part of it; nor may it require that 'provision of any particular kind should be made in school timetables (Section 4(3)). Advice may be given by the Schools Curriculum Council and the School Examinations and Assessment Council (also established by the Act) on matters such as these, but the advice will be in the form of guidance and not a statutory requirement upon schools. These points are reinforced in *From Policy to Practice*,[18] which points out that the organization of the curriculum to deliver national requirements and support LEAs' and governors' curricular policies is a matter for the headteacher. The attainment targets and programmes of study do, however, reflect general assumptions about appropriate amounts of time required by the subjects.

It will be particularly important to remember these points when filling in the table which will be attached to Form 7[19] and will have to be returned by schools each January showing the time spent on various aspects of the curriculum, including the National

Curriculum. I am not surprised that the DES and Welsh Office want such information so as to consider how the National Curriculum is working and what modifications, if any, are required in it. Furthermore, I would not be surprised if the total amount of 'time' added up to more than 100 per cent. In both primary and secondary schools work is done that simultaneously contributes to more than one of the Foundation Subjects. The distinction between the timetable and the curriculum must again be stressed.

For the purposes of the National Curriculum, the compulsory years of schooling are divided into four key stages related to the traditional divisions of infant (5–7), junior (7–11), lower secondary (11–14) and upper secondary (14–16). Assessment for reporting purposes under the National Curriculum will take place towards the end of each key stage. The key stages will be the same irrespective of the ages at which children change from one phase to another in a locality, though what is proposed is undoubtedly adding another doubt to the continued existence of first and middle schools.

In line with the earlier Government papers on the curriculum, traditional subjects names are used as the headings under which to describe the curriculum. They are all called Foundation Subjects and the full list for key stages 1 and 2 was given on page 46.

Attainment Targets

One of the hoped-for gains from the National Curriculum was that the terms used to talk and write about the curriculum would be common all over England and Wales, and have standard meanings — rather as standard measures once had to be defined. Whether uniformity of use has yet been achieved for the term 'attainment targets' is doubtful. In the 1988 Act, Part 1, Section 2, subsection 2(a) says that 'the knowledge, skills and understanding which pupils of different abilities and maturities are expected to have by the end of each key stage' are referred to as 'attainment targets'.

However, the Education (National Curriculum) (Attainment Targets and Programmes of Study in Science) Order laid before

Parliament in March, 1989, includes as Attainment Target 2 (to choose but one example from but one subject):

> Pupils should develop their knowledge and understanding of the diversity and classification of past and present life-forms, and of the relationships, energy, flows, cycles of matter and human influences within ecosystems.

That Attainment Target is then interpreted through successive 'statements of attainment' divided into 10 levels and intended to cover all children between 5 and 16, i.e. in all four key stages. For example, by the end of Level 1:

> know that there is a wide variety of living things, which includes human beings.

and at Level 10:

> understand predator-prey relationships in the context of managed eco-systems.
>
> understand how materials for growth and energy are transferred through an eco-system.

In the Order, the Attainment Target is a pathway of learning which, as in this case, may have no end, it is not something a pupil can 'have' by the end of a key stage. On the other hand, one may set markers along the pathway by which progress can be judged, as has been done through the statements of attainment, which fit more closely the definition of Attainment Targets used in the Act. We have the same confusion that we have had for years between aims and objectives — which surely ought, respectively, to mean 'directions of travel' and 'points to be reached' but are often used interchangeably. Perhaps we can hope that the confusion will be cleared up when the Act is adjusted in the light of experience of it. *From Policy to Practice* brings out the uncertainty of definition when it refers to Attainment Targets as covering 'the range of knowledge, skills and understanding which pupils should be expected and helped to master as they progress through school . . . setting out areas within which pupils will need to develop their attainments'.

Programmes of Study

The Act uses the term 'programmes of study' to refer to:

> the matters, skills and processes which are required to be taught to pupils of different abilities and maturities during each key stage.

Anxiety has been expressed by a number of people that the notion of progression which underlies the Act is too simple and that it does not fit the ways in which children learn: it is thought to be too linear by far. The warning must be taken seriously, and it would be wholly justified if the definitions of progression and the steps in the programmes of study were numerous and small, and that progression was interpreted as a single line of development in a subject, let alone for the curriculum as a unity. I shall return to this issue when discussing assessment, but it is apposite here that the pathways — the attainment targets — are relatively many while the stages and 'levels' along them are relatively few. This combination should allow considerable interweaving as individual children make progress. The critics, in my view, are falling into the trap of expecting the results to be more precise than current knowledge of children and learning permit and the practicalities of teaching allow.

Are There Dangers?

The obvious answer must be 'yes'. Of course, there are dangers in everything we do. The food we eat, the liquids we drink, the air we breathe may all be contaminated. The journeys we make may end in maiming and even fatal accidents. Not to eat, drink or breathe will bring an even swifter end, and not to travel would be to miss many opportunities for pleasure, knowledge, wonder and enjoyment. If the main purpose of a National Curriculum is clear, that it is to improve the chance that each child will have an education that enables him or her to put the most into and get the best out of life, then the more serious dangers should be avoided and the gains realized. The implications are that regard must be paid to the differences between children and their circumstances, and use made of local opportunities for teaching and learning. The schools and the teachers should make the detailed choice of the illustrations to be used in developing children's skills, concepts and attitudinal percepts. I say 'detailed choice of illustrations' because some general obligations upon schools are necessary and I believe acceptable to schools: I cannot conceive of an adequate education that made no reference to the ways people live in other parts of the world, or made no use of literature. The fact that Parliament decrees the obligation also places upon Parliament the duty to ensure the availability of the resources necessary to the conduct of the programmes.

As is well known, children of the same age or key stage differ in their backgrounds and their current abilities. Children change as they grow older. The danger that arises when the curriculum is described in subject terms is that the definitions of the subjects will be suited to work done by older children but not be what is appropriate and necessary for younger children. I have already commented on the difficulty of finding a place in the subject scheme for handwriting and even reading, and the undesirable effect of regarding those as aspects of teaching the English language. Geography and history are equally at risk. Both need to encompass those time-consuming and instructive processes through which teachers introduce 4- or 5-year-old children to the unfamiliar, larger community of a school where the chance of getting quick and substantial attention from an adult is reduced. Even the geography of the school is more complex than the geography of the home and early lessons in the subject involve making the link between tiles on the floor, taps on the wall and activities that use liquids. Early lessons in history, geography and moral education concern the rules by which people, mostly children, group and regroup for different purposes. Both the definitions of the subjects and the interpretations of the definitions must allow for children who are inexperienced and immature even as compared with other 5-year-olds. The first key stage is for these as well as for 7-year-olds. Indeed, although the first key stage is for children who, chronologically, are of compulsory school age, some of their number could easily be mistaken for 2- or 3-year-olds in one or more aspects of their behaviour: in their control of hands and fingers; in their speech; in their ability to wait their turn; and so on. If the National Curriculum cannot acknowledge the time, space and hard work that has to go into teaching those children, then it will be built on sand. On the other hand, if, for the first time, the value of that work is given its proper recognition, the gains will be considerable.

Some of the most difficult issues are connected with the assessment of children and the publication of schools' results. They are the concern of the next Chapter.

Notes

1. DES/HMI (1980) *Matters for Discussion, A View of the Curriculum*, London, HMSO.
2. DES/HMI (1978) *Primary Education in England*, London, HMSO.
3. DES/WO (1980) *A Framework for the School Curriculum*, London, HMSO.
4. DES/WO (1981) *The School Curriculum*, London, HMSO.
5. DES (1986) *Local Authority Policies for the School Curriculum, Report on the Circular 8/83 Review*, London, DES.
6. DES (1983) Cmnd. 8836 *Teaching Quality*, London, HMSO.
7. DES (1985) Cmnd. 9469 *Better Schools*, London, HMSO.
8. A rather different view is taken in *Better Schools* (DES (1985)) which recognizes in Paragraph 152 that primary school teachers have the strongest claim for additional time.
9. DES/HMI (1982) *The New Teacher in School*, London, HMSO.
10. DES/WO (1985) *Science 5–16: A statement of policy*, London and Cardiff, DES and Welsh Office.
11. DES (1986) *Local Authority Policies for the School Curriculum, op. cit.*
12. House of Commons Education, Science and Arts Committee (1986) *Achievement in Primary Schools*, Third Report, Session 1985–86: HC 40–I, Volume 1, London, HMSO.
13. DES/WO (1985) *Science 5–16, op. cit.*

14. DES/HMI (1985) *The Curriculum from 5 to 16: Curriculum Matters 2*, London, HMSO.
15. DES/WO (1987) *The National Curriculum 5–16, a consultation document*, London, DES.
16. Haviland, J. (1988) *Take Care, Mr Baker!*, p. 1, viii, London, Fourth Estate.
17. Education Reform Act (1988) London, HMSO.
18. DES (1989) *The National Curriculum: From Policy to Practice* paragraph 4.3, London, DES.
19. Form 7 is an annual return made by every maintained school to the DES giving information about the numbers of pupils, teachers, and the ways pupils are grouped.

Chapter 7

Assessment and Accountability

What children do at school has been assessed ever since the first school was formed. Assessment is an essential part of teaching. As the House of Commons Select Committee put it:

> the skills of diagnosing learning success and difficulty and selecting and presenting new tasks are the essence of the teachers' profession and vital to children's progress.[1]

Assessment Has Four Main Forms.

1. Overwhelmingly, assessment is relatively detailed, informal and undertaken in the course of the day's work. Assessment of this kind is probably one of the most difficult parts of a teacher's job, but far less time is given to it in initial training and in in-service training than is given to discussing child development in general terms. For the purposes of this chapter, I shall call this aspect of assessment *informal assessment*.

Sometimes more formal processes are used. They have been of two kinds:

2. Special exercises may be devised and set by the teacher or by people who may never have seen children who work them. When they are set, the teacher and children know

that the occasion is special in that the process of teaching is abandoned for the time being. The children must rely on their own resources and expect no help. I shall call these '*tests*', though the definition includes examinations, which are more substantial. Commercially produced tests may be normative tests, or diagnostic tests, or a combination of the two. It will be helpful in what follows to keep in mind some of the characteristics of these tests. They may be 'objective', in the sense that anyone marking them brings no personal judgement to bear except to be satisfied whether or not the answers correspond to what the makers of the test say are right. They are also likely to be standardized in two senses. First, the form in which the test is presented is laid down and must be adhered to, and secondly, the scores obtained by children now taking the test can be compared with an initial group chosen to represent some wider population, for example, to be representative of all 9-year-olds in England. Like all tests, and indeed all measurement, the results obtained from them are subject to uncertainties. In these cases, the original sample cannot, except by the remotest chance, be exactly like the whole population it is said to represent. The items chosen for the test will not precisely represent the general skill or concept which is under examination, i.e. the *validity* of the test will not be perfect. Again as with all pieces of work done, the performance of any child or group of children will not be exactly the same from one occasion to the next, even allowing for maturation and teaching in between, i.e. the test's *reliability* will not be perfect. The test constructors strive to keep the uncertainties to a minimum, but some still inevitably remain even on the day the test is published. They may be compounded because the test is used, or its results are interpreted erroneously in ways that we shall come to. Furthermore, tests age and life outside changes. When one of the tests used in national surveys of reading was constructed, 'mannequins' were people who paraded at exhibitions of new clothes; by the time it was last used, such people were 'models'.

3. Teachers think about a child's work over a period, a week or a term or a year, and enter their assessments (or it can be examples of a child's work) in a 'permanent' record. When doing so they may take account of their informal assessments and the results of tests. I shall call these *'summary assessments'*.

All three of these forms of assessment were common in primary schools when the Plowden Report was published and are likely to persist, but another is being prepared:

4. The fourth kind is being developed for the National Curriculum. These will be Standard Assessment Tasks or SATs, which ought not to look like tests to the children and should, like teachers' informal assessments, be concerned with identifying what children can do and not, in the first place at least, with their relative placings. In some ways they may look like mini-schemes of work. They will be standardized in the sense that they should be presented and marked in prescribed ways.

The Purposes of Assessment.

To Inform the Current Teacher

The main purpose of informal assessment is to enable a teacher to decide what a child should do next. A teacher's conclusions about a child's ability might lead in very different directions.

One of the simpler judgements to make is whether a child is competent at finding the difference between one number and another providing the larger is under 100. There are actually a number of complications that we need not go into here, but let us suppose the teacher decides that one child cannot and another can. What then? The first child's errors need careful examination to discover what their causes might be. Teaching and practice then have to be chosen that will help the child overcome what is proving difficult. The possibilities are many. They may even have little to do with arithmetic and much to do with handwriting and orderliness of layout. They may show that the child has lost sight of the fact that two whole quantities are being dealt with and is blinded by a rote methodology that concentrates on the digits which make up the numbers. Whatever the teacher's conclusion, the process of understanding the difficulty is the one known as diagnosis and is concerned with gap filling. It is a highly skilled business and is likely to remain so even with the coming of computer programmes that aid diagnosis, as for example that devised by the NFER on addition and subtraction, described by Graham Ruddock.[2]

The fact that a computer programme can be drawn up indicates that there is some consistency in the errors children make. In the same article, Ruddock outlines a more generalized approach to the diagnosis of error. The NFER has been responsible for the Assessment of Performance Unit studies of nationwide achievement in mathematics. From those there is ample evidence of what some 11-year-olds find relatively easy and others find difficult. In decimal notation, fractions, symmetry, ratio, area, volume and geometry, high attainers differ from lower attainers, not just the lowest, because they have a better grasp of the concepts involved rather than because they are more skilled. As Ruddock says, 'there is food for thought here for the back-to-basics movement, and for those who ignore the disastrous experience with minimum competency testing across the Atlantic. Diagnosis of this kind points to issues that must be taken up in general teaching practices, in initial and in-service training, in which the development of teachers' individual skills of diagnosis should play a larger part.

But what of the child who can do what was asked? There are three types of action that might follow. The first is the one that is probably taken too often and leads to HMI's complaints that children are doing less difficult work than they could manage: under-expectation is identified. It is to get the child to do more of the same. One reason why this happens is that the teacher is feeling hard pressed by other children who need a lot of help, and it is something of a relief to have some members of the class who can get on by themselves for a time. Within limits that is a reasonable line to take in the interests of class management[3] and as a way of making it possible to assess all children in the course of their work as well as assessing the product of it. As with so many other things that are acceptable it becomes harmful when over-used. Either all of the children spend a lot of time practising what they can already do, or a few do, usually the children who are making the quickest progress. The last is hard both on the quicker, since their progress is unduly slowed, and also on the less advanced, since they are continually expected to be tackling things that are difficult for them. But children are also given work they can already manage so that their performance becomes more highly polished or speedier, or on the grounds that they need to 'overlearn' so that they will not forget when next the skill or idea comes in useful. As with so many other things in teaching, there is a balance to be struck and it is important to keep practice under critical review so that the rut in which one travels does not become circular.

A second course of next action is to provide the child with more difficult work of the same kind, using the skills and ideas already developed and extending them. That is a fairly straightforward action, though it requires the teacher to be aware of what might come next. In subtraction that is relatively easy to decide, though there are pitfalls. In developing a child's interest in literature, for example, it may be harder: the judgements that have to be made are about the child's interests as well as about his or her reading ability, and even in that the demands made by a book are not easy to identify; extensive knowledge of what is currently available is not in every teacher's head; and there should be room for choice by the child whose mood and preference, like that of any adult, vary from time to time.

A third course of action is to move the child onto something quite different. It may be in the same National Curriculum subject but in another attainment target. It might on another occasion be quite a different subject or outside the National Curriculum. That kind of shift calls for assessment that goes beyond the matter immediately in hand. It requires a view about the achievements of the child across the range of learning, and about the relationships between different aspects of learning. The teacher must have a profile of expectations as well as an understanding of the child's profile of achievement. We come again to the question of balance in learning and balance in the curriculum, which is sure to show unevenness in any child.[4]

To Inform the Children

When teachers make an assessment of a piece of work done by a child they frequently let the child know what they think of it. Sometimes the message is simple and clear: ten sums right out of 15; three words spelt wrongly out of 153 (it can look as though the only words that matter are the ones spelt wrong). At other times the message is more complex and may be quite difficult to interpret. Suppose the child has written a story and the teacher writes 'Good' beneath it. What does that mean? Does it mean that the spelling, syntax and the construction and content of the story were all good? Good by what standards? Were they good by reference to children of the same age throughout England; or by reference to children in this school or class; or by reference to what this child has done in the past; or by reference to what the teacher hoped for when the piece of work was set? Marten Shipman[5] has discussed this issue lucidly and in greater detail elsewhere.

To Inform Others About Individual Children

Assessment by a teacher for purposes that are to be pursued within the class are certainly enriched by knowledge of what is being achieved elsewhere, but some variation is acceptable and even inevitable providing the judgements are broadly consistent and understood by the people involved. Idiosyncrasy also happens when teachers' immediate experience unduly colours their general perceptions. If swans become geese, that is a bar to communication when the results of assessment have to be reported to others. Language, including numbers, has to be used with as nearly common meanings as possible by those engaged in the dialogue. The difficulty is just like the one that had to be overcome by establishing what would count as an inch throughout the Kingdom. In educational assessment, which is far more complex than measuring length, standardization has presented some difficulties. It has led to the use of increasing numbers of standardized tests devised by people who spend their lives grappling with the problems and making the tests, though corelation between tests is less than perfect.

Parents

When parents ask how their child is getting on they may not have thought through the possible interpretations of their question, or they may feel that it would be discourteous to be more probing. Either way, the answer may cause confusion if its reference points are not clear. The difficulties are much the same as those outlined earlier when referring to comments made to children. There was plenty of evidence that confusion occurred among Inner London parents[6] who had been told that their children had been doing well throughout the primary school only to discover that they were put in the lowest of three bands for the purpose of allocation to secondary schools. It seems reasonable to suppose that the teachers had answered the questions, 'Is my child trying hard and making as much progress as can be expected? Should I be pleased with him or her?'

Some teachers worry that parents might put counterproductive pressure on a child and it would be surprising if there were none such. It is highly doubtful whether, in the long run and taking all parents together, there is gain in keeping back the answer to the other half of the parents' question: 'How is my child doing for his or her age?' That question requires a national reference point.

The next teacher(s)

One notable form of assessment that has reduced in volume is the 11-plus selection system to decide whether a child should go to a grammar school or to a secondary modern school. I doubt whether the public ever realized how unevenly the process operated from one LEA to another, even within some LEAs, and as between boys and girls. The proportion of children going on to grammar schools in England and Wales varied from under 20 per cent to over 40 per cent and with no corelation between the percentages and the general affluence of the locality. Where there were potentially equal numbers of places available to boys and girls, the sexes were often listed separately and a 'borderline' girl had to score more on the tests than did a 'borderline' boy to get a grammar school place. One argument put forward for this was that boys in the end did better. A curious argument to put alongside the idea that the object of the 11-plus system was to predict later performance. Experience of streaming within schools indicates how difficult it is to transfer children between streams, especially downwards. It proved even more difficult between schools, and the only significant movement was of some children into the Sixth Forms of grammar schools. The secondary modern schools gradually began to aim towards the public examinations at 16 and some children who 'failed' their 11-plus went on to do better at the General Certificate of Education examination than some others who had been placed in grammar schools. This is not the place to discuss secondary education, and my purpose in raising the issue is to draw attention again to the impossibility of putting children into a single order of educational merit; the statisticians' calculation that some 20 per cent of children are misplaced in such a selection process should be taken seriously. If the children, their parents and the public at large believe that the order of alleged merit is more than an approximation, then a disservice is being done to some children and unhappiness unfairly created in some families. Additionally, there is a warning about the unevenness of progress from child to child.

There remains a need to inform the next teacher or teachers about the children they will be taking on. Many attempts have been made to devise improved systems of recording pupils' progress. The Schools Council funded a project on the issue which was led by P. S. Clift.[7] The team came to the conclusions that the systems that worked best were those that had been arranged by the people actually using them and that grew out of decisions and agreement about the curriculum. They thought that was one reason why teachers so often found LEA record systems unsatisfactory. Useful records should give clear indications about future teaching needs and distinguish those judgements from descriptions of children's educational experience. It was vital that teachers should have the time to keep written records and discuss their findings with other teachers in their own and other schools as needed. The implications for continuous assessment under the National Curriculum are clear. The fact that the curriculum is, to that extent, common ought to make a more satisfactory recording system possible. But it will require time for recording and consultation between teachers if it is to be of any use.

Educational psychologists

Reports sometimes have to be made to educational psychologists and perhaps to people in the medical services. These ordinarily have to be standardized in form, at least in part. They may be special reports on individuals, but they have also been part of a more comprehensive collection of information about the achievements of all of the children in some LEAs.

To Provide Information to the Public

During the years between the Plowden Report and the National Curriculum there was a growing interest in the performance of the education system as a whole, nationally and in an LEA, and of the performance of individual schools. The opinions expressed, some based on evidence, varied. For a time there was a growth in the view that schools were unable to reduce the individual differences between children; it is doubtful whether that view ever captured more than an esoteric audience. It was counterbalanced by research — the statistics have been questioned — on a group of secondary schools by Michael Rutter,[8] and more recently by Peter Mortimer *et al.* in *School Matters*,[9] David Smith and Sally Tomlinson[10] and by Harvey

Goldstein and Desmond Nuttal,[11] that schools do make a difference, some being more effective than others.

Another view, conveyed especially by the Black Papers,[12] was that schools could make a difference and that they had generally got worse at doing so, partly due to comprehensive secondary schooling but also because of 'progressive' primary education. A third view, which I regard as more soundly based, came out of the HMI survey of primary education[13] and national surveys of reading and other aspects of learning by the Assessment of Performance Unit. It was that primary school children's performance in reading had improved, but that with a reasonably broad curriculum further general improvement was possible and necessary — a view confirmed by the ORACLE research of Brian Simon, Maurice Galton and others at Leicester University.

One case, that of the William Tyndale Junior School, played an especially important part in shaping public opinion and attitudes. Professional opinion among the teachers in the school was split about the efficacy of the organization and methods of teaching being used by some of their number. The relationships were strained to breaking point between some school managers and some of the teachers, including the headteacher. The relationships between the school managers, or at least some of them, and the ILEA were fractious. Robin Auld's[14] report made it clear that two contributing factors that led to a breakdown of communication and a failure to act were that the powers of the Managers were weak in the extreme and required goodwill and trust if they were to operate; and that no-one in the LEA had a synoptic view of what was happening and also could determine action.

Even while the William Tyndale Junior School was providing copy for national newspapers, there was a national committee[15] deliberating on the management of schools. Detailed discussion of the latter's findings are outside the scope of this book. What is of interest here is that the publicity given to the Tyndale affair increased the inclination of many to want to know what was going on in schools, to know how well the children were achieving and to consider how the management of schools could be modified to bring changes about.

The Increase in LEA Testing

Writing in 1981, Caroline Gipps and Robert Wood[16] referred to changes that had occurred in testing since the publication of the Bullock Report. LEAs were less inclined to use tests in which children are asked to read a series of unconnected words, like the Schonell Graded Word Reading Test, though teachers, perhaps those who emphasized a phonic approach, still regarded them highly. Group tests had become more popular than individual reading tests, with about a third of LEAs using the Young's Group Reading Test, though there were said to be shortcomings in its standardization for children over 10. They reported that the testing of reading by LEAs was spread throughout primary schools with 7 being the most popular age both in the Bullock survey (28 LEAs) and in theirs (57 LEAs). Taking all ages together, the incidence of testing in primary schools rose from 57 in the Bullock survey to 114[17] in the Enquiry into the Use of Test Result for Accountability Purposes (ETSP) survey.[18] It has to be remembered that there were fewer LEAs at the time of the ETSP survey (104, of whom 88 completed the questionnaire) than at the time of the Bullock survey (146, of whom 93 responded), so one test applied in the second survey may have involved more schools and more children than one applied in the first.

ETSP found that the purposes of testing were often not well thought of. For example, the Neale test was used too late in a child's infant school period to allow that school to use the diagnostic information in its work, and the junior school was given only the reading accuracy scores when they would also have liked to know how well the children could comprehend what they read. One reason for choosing a particular test or set of tests (the case referred to concerned the Edinburgh tests), was that its use would broaden teachers' perceptions of what reading included, though at the expense of the longer time it took to apply it as compared with some others.

The Uses To Which Test Results Are Put

There are probably five main reasons why LEAs use and choose tests, though it would be rare for all to occur together and in some cases none is clearly articulated nor its consequences followed through:

A first is to provide the elected members and possibly the public with information about the quality of education in the Authority's area. The information so provided is crude, though it probably was the best objective evidence available before what is promised by the National Curriculum. The problem is that the information may mislead because it seems to be more precise than the tests used actually warrant, or because the local population is not sufficiently comparable with the sample of children on whom that test was standardized: the results may produce unwarranted complacency or a false depression. The mean score will inevitably fluctuate from one occasion to another but the differences over one year, and even over five years, may well be small and both statistically and educationally insignificant. Many people unused to interpreting such figures will make too much of such changes.

A second is to provide information that will help in the transfer of pupils from primary schools to secondary schools. This can happen in areas where there is selection at 11 or 12 with children going to grammar or secondary modern schools, or whatever their local designations are. It can also contribute, as it did in the ILEA, to arranging that each school has an intake that extends across the ability range. No-one should suppose that the system is precise. In the case of the ILEA, the results of the test were used to tell a school approximately how many of its pupils, not which pupils, would be in each of the three bands.

A third is to influence teaching, either to make it broader as in the case quoted above or, by highlighting reading and mathematics, to persuade the teachers to increase the time children spend on practising examples of the kind used in the tests. As the 1978 HMI survey of primary education showed, and as has been repeated many times in DES publications since, that is not the most effective way to improve children's abilities in reading and mathematics. They need to face a more extensive and demanding range of applications.

A fourth is to identify schools that are achieving unsatisfactorily. The problem of identifying unsatisfactory schools is real enough. Test results can give warning that a school should be looked at more closely. It has to be remembered that the warning could be signalled by a higher than average score in national terms if the school is in an affluent area. There ought to be other and earlier warning signs like a high turnover, or very low turnover of staff (neither is a certain danger sign), or complaints from parents, poor take-up of in-service training opportunities, or worries of LEA advisers or inspectors arising from their visits. The score, however expressed, is not enough by itself. It is very doubtful whether there is advantage in an LEA publicly naming schools because they are failing, a practice adopted latterly by the ILEA; the public may need to be informed of action the LEA takes to remedy the failure, but that is a different matter.

A fifth is to identify children who are failing and who need extra help that the LEA can provide. There is a difficulty in allocating extra resources to some schools and not others. The children's needs should be paramount, not the ability of the headteacher to persuade those who control the distribution of resources, or the reluctance of a teacher to initiate action: a system of choosing between the claims of different schools is desirable. For that, either one person has to see the children in question and decide among them or a system has to be devised that teachers in all the schools can administer in such a way that the results are reasonably consistent from school to school. Even when one person decides, moving from school to school, it is probably an advantage if the process can be objective and standardized, though it is doubtful whether it needs to be norm-referenced. It is desirable that it should be diagnostic so that it contributes to decisions about what teaching is required by each of the children. This purpose does not essentially require testing all of the children in an age group in an LEA area when only a small proportion, well known to their teachers, form the border group to be considered. The question put to the teachers should not be, 'Which of your pupils need special help?', but rather, 'Which four (or some other suitable number) of your children find most difficulty in learning to read (or whatever service is being offered)?' The moderation could begin with those, though in some schools it may prove necessary to consider more than the four first identified if all are found to be in special need.

It now needs to be asked whether these five purposes could and should be met by assessment conducted for the National Curriculum. If they can be, as I believe, then the previous pattern of LEA testing should be redundant.

The Identification of Children with Special Needs

The identification of children with special educational needs had two strands up to the mid-1960s. One was concerned almost exclusively with children who were and would continue to be taught in ordinary, now called mainstream, schools, but who were having difficulty in learning to read or with mathematics, though the second was taken into account much less often than the first. The other was the identification of children in mainstream schools who were better suited to education in special units attached to mainstream schools or in special schools. The latter were defined in terms of their handicaps: mental, physical, sensory or behavioural. The two strands were brought together in the report of the Warnock Committee,[19] which much influenced the 1981 Education Act. The Report made a far reaching revision of the definition of special need in proposing that it should be defined in terms of the educational requirements of the child and not in terms of the child's handicap. The Committee presumed that about 20 per cent of children would require special educational treatment at some time during their schooling, and about 15 per cent would be in need at any one time. Of course, the percentages may be larger or smaller in any one school.

The change in the way of defining need is important because it requires a positive definition of the action to be taken instead of a negative description of what the child cannot do (compare, as a matter of interest, this approach with the ILEA decision to name poor schools). Some children need teaching and resources that are outside what the school can manage from its ordinary resources, including access to an area remedial service. They may require special equipment (like a loop-transmission system in the classroom that will transmit the teacher's voice to a deaf child), or the provision of an ancillary worker to care specifically for a child with spina bifida. Or they may require, for a short time or longer, a place in a school specifically provided to meet the needs of a group of children with similar needs. Their identification is subject to a process which requires consultation between teachers, the educational psychologist, the medical services and others who may have a contribution to make, especially the child's parents. The result is a statement of educational need.

The increase in the number of children in mainstream schools who need highly specific support and teaching and a formal statement of need is probably as much due to the changing attitudes towards children with special educational needs as it is to the 1981 Act.

There remain children who should have more support and probably more personal attention than most of their age but who can be provided for out of the ordinary resources of the school plus, possibly, help from the remedial service. A change that may be gathering momentum as the 1990s replace the 1980s is that the activities of those in the remedial support services are being directed more at the teacher and less at the child. It was the case that peripatetic remedial teachers moved from school to school, teaching small groups of children drawn from one or more classes. It was extremely difficult for the work done to be interlocked with the work the child did for the rest of the day and week, even in the aspect, usually reading, causing the anxiety. The newer arrangements should be more effective if it is possible for the regular class-teacher, or another regular teacher in the school, to give sufficient time to the children who need it and in such a way that the efforts made, by teacher and children, both contribute to and draw from the full range of teaching and learning to which the children are subject.

There will continue to be a need to adjudicate between children in different schools for the resources available. Though some help should come from the money held back by LEAs when distributing funds under the arrangements for the local management of schools, it is certainly necessary to take the differences between school populations into account in the formulas that distribute funds to them. Three-quarters of the funds available for schools will be distributed according to the numbers and ages of pupils. The remaining 25 per cent will take a number of factors into account, including special local factors. The assessment arrangements under the National Curriculum ought to provide information to assist distribution, and if the intentions are translated effectively at each stage, from the School Examinations and Assessment Council to the individual teacher, the standard framework they provide should make largely redundant the use of standardized tests of the old sort.

Notes

1. House of Commons Education, Science and Arts Committe (1986) *Achievement in Primary Schools*, Third Report, Session 1985–86: HC 40–I., paragraph 7.23, London, HMSO.
2. Ruddock, G. (1988) *Diagnostic Testing and Primary Mathematics*, in *Issues in Primary Education: Recent Research*, produced for NFER Members' Conference, Slough, NFER.
3. For a vivid description of a teacher's difficulty in assessing a child in

action, see Desforges, C. (1984) *Understanding the quality of pupil learning experience* in Entwhistle, N. (Ed.) *New Directions in Educational Psychology I: Learning and Teaching*, Lewes, Falmer Press.

4. See also Chapter 2.
5. Shipman, M. (1983) *Assessment in Primary and Middle Schools*, London, Croom Helm.
6. ILEA (1985) *Improving Primary Schools*, London, ILEA.
7. Clift, P. S., Weiner, G. G. and Wilson, E. L. (1981) *Record Keeping in Primary Schools*, London, Macmillan.
8. Rutter, M., Maugham, B., Mortimore, P. and Ouston, J. (1979) *Fifteen Thousand Hours*, London, Open Books.
9. Mortimer, P., Sammons, P., Stoll, L., Lewis, D. and Ecob, R. (1988) *School Matters: The Junior Years*, Wells, Open Book Publishers.
10. Smith, D. and Tomlinson, S. (1989) *The Second Effect: A Study of Multi-Racial Comprehensives*, London, Policy Studies Institute.
11. Goldstein, H. and Nuttall, D. (4 July 1989) *Education Guardian: Screen Tests for Progress*, London, Guardian Newspapers.
12. Cox, C. B. and Dyson, A. E. (Eds) (1969) *Black Papers*, London, The Critical Quarterly Society.
13. DES/HMI (1978) *Primary Education in England*, London, HMSO.
14. Auld, R. (1979) *William Tyndale Junior and Infant Schools: Public Enquiry*, London, ILEA.
15. DES (1977) *A New Partnership in Our Schools*, London, HMSO.
16. Gipps, C. and Wood, R. (1981) *The Testing of Reading in LEAs: the Bullock Report seven years on*, in *Educational Studies* Vol. 2, Abingdon, Carfax Publications Co.
17. These figures should be treated as no more than general guides because the LEAs had been reorganized between the two surveys, the response rates were not the same, and it is not certain from the table given whether the testing of the 11 + age group was all in the middle or secondary schools. Some LEAs tested at more than one age, hence the use of the word 'incidences' when referring to all ages together.
18. Gipps, C. (1983) *Testing Children: standardised testing in local education authorities and schools*, Oxford, Heinemann Educational.
19. Warnock, H. M. (1978) *Special Educational Needs*, London, HMSO.

Chapter 8

The National Curriculum and Assessment

In preparing for the National Curriculum, the Secretary of State set up the Task Group on Assessment and Testing (TGAT), chaired by Paul Black. The Group produced a main report, supplementary reports and a digest for schools.[1] TGAT proposed that assessment related to the National Curriculum should be *criterion-referenced* in the sense that the concern should be to describe what a child can do rather than, primarily, to compare one child with others. The assessment should be *formative*, indicating where a child was in a continuing process of learning, so providing information about what should be done next to help the child forward; except that for 16-year-olds the assessment would be summative, showing what a child had achieved through his or her school years. It took the definition of attainment targets as given — as directions of travel rather than as points to be reached — and proposed that work in these should be divided into 10 levels, presumed to cover the whole period from 5 to 16 and all children. Everyone would begin school in Level 1. Most children would take two years to work through a level, but some would go more slowly and others more quickly, hence the need to have 10 levels. The assumption was that for the present if not forever, the range of achievement in an aspect of the curriculum would be much the same as now, i.e. the equivalent of about '7 years' at 11. By the end of Key Stage 1, some children would still be in Level 1, most would have moved through to Level 2, and some to Level 3. At the end of Key Stage 2, nearly everyone would be in Levels 3 to 5.

The assessment should be related to *profile components*. These would be combinations of attainment targets, and change in their composition from one level to another. The argument was that there would be too many attainment targets for each to be dealt with separately in reporting (there are 33 in the three core subjects). Those that were compatible should be combined. However, it would generally be unwise to combine for a whole subject since a child might show significant differences of achievement in different parts of the subject. It would be meaningless to combine the assessments from whole subjects into a single aggregate or average either for a child or for a school.

The results of assessment of individual children should be made available to those who needed to have them: to parents, to appropriate teachers and members of the LEA staff. They should not be publicly available. The results for schools should be published from the end of Key Stage 2 by the schools themselves as part of their brochures. The information should show the distribution of pupils Level by Level and profile component by profile component. The LEA should provide information for inclusion in the brochure that would indicate the effects of the nature of the catchment area on results. Schools should not be required to publish the results for Key Stage 1 because they would be particularly susceptible to the variety of pre-school experience that children have, and to the various lengths of their infant schooling.

The basis of assessment should be continuous assessment by teachers. Clearly these might be affected by the limitations of the current experience of individual teachers and so a method of standardization was proposed. This had two parts: at the ends of Key Stages 1 and 2 (effectively the ends of the infant and junior stages) the children should work through Standard Assessment Tasks (SATS); at the end of Key Stage 2 it might also be necessary for children to take specific tests. The SATS ought to appear to the children as ordinary pieces of work, covering a number of different aspects of the curriculum. There should be three at the end of Key Stage 1 and four at the end of Key Stage 2. The teachers would choose the SATS, with an exception we shall come to in a moment, from a national bank of SATS so that the subject matter would be suited to the children. They would be presented and the children's work assessed according to instructions provided with the SATS.

The second part of the procedure for coordinating assessment across schools was to be a moderation procedure. This would bring teachers together from a number of schools, say 12 to 15, who would compare their assessments with each other and, more particularly, consider the relationship between the spread of results obtained from continuous assessment and those obtained from the SATS. The group of teachers — and this is the exception referred to earlier — would have chosen one of the SATS to use in all schools in the moderating group so that there would be a common base for discussion.

There are a number of important consequences of using a moderation system of this kind. It is possible to be more adventurous in the form of the SATS than if they were to be the final decider in the assessment of individuals. Any practicable system has to balance excellent performance in some attainment targets against mediocre performance in others, and the moderating groups could establish sensible balances with the help of broad guidelines from the School Examinations and Assessment Council (SEAC). The groups would provide a system for feedback to SEAC about the suitability of SATS and the system in general. They would provide a new and vitally important opportunity for in-service development in the assessment of children's work, and could be the most significant element in the National Curriculum in improving the quality of education.

The intention of TGAT was that differences in the results from continuous assessment and the SATS should be resolved as a result of the work of the moderating groups: sometimes a teacher would have to balance out the results of continuous assessments to produce the same pattern as the SATS had revealed; sometimes the revision might be somewhere between the two; sometimes it might be concluded that the SATS were wrong and action was required by SEAC rather than by the teachers.

Changes Proposed by SEAC

The TGAT proposals were broadly accepted by the Secretary of State.[2] There were some obvious anxieties about the cost of the moderating system. The then Secretary of State made it known that he would like schools to publish results at the end of Key Stage 1, but the Education Reform Act does not require them to do so.

SEAC has now written[3] to the Secretary of State expressing its view on the National Curriculum Assessment Arrangements, promising further recommendations in December, 1989. What SEAC proposes retains the idea that assessment should be criterion-referenced. It retains the idea that the results should not be aggregated across the curriculum as a whole. From there on, there are significant shifts. Some appear to be attached to the earlier fears expressed about the costs of full moderation. Some arise because of the differences of approach between one Subject Working Group and another, and the different levels of understanding about what a profile component, in TGAT terms, comprises.

I take them one at a time.

The Accommodation between Teachers' Assessments (TA) and SATS

I shall use the term Teachers' Assessment as used by SEAC. It is part of what TGAT called continuous assessment.

The proposal is to use achievement in an attainment target as 'the basic building block' of assessment for recording and reporting purposes. Reports to parents should make available information about children's achievements in the attainment targets, the profile components and each subject. It should be remembered that English, Science, Mathematics and Technology have between them produced 41 attainment targets. A primary school teacher with 30 children in the class will have to have information ready to provide 1230 assessments which will be sent forward to the moderating group. More attainment targets are to come for other subjects.

I believe that we should make a distinction between assessment for internal school and teaching practices on the one hand, and assessment for external recording and publication purposes on the other. Teachers need to consider detail when deciding what children should go on to do. They need — as in the past — to work at something like the detail implied not only by attainment targets, but also at the finer detail of statements of attainment. For example, to assess whether (and in what circumstances) a child can 'describe what has happened in a story and predict what may happen next', is merely one of six statements of attainment at Level 2 in Attainment Target 2 in English. Such detail about every aspect of learning, if used for external purposes, will produce a mass of information that is beyond anyone's ability to comprehend or to deal with. Indeed, I doubt if the cost of recording and storing the information would anywhere near justify its collection. Sometimes, when there is something interesting to say or to consider, it may be necessary to go into the detail, but those cases are likely to be relatively few. Profile components would provide enough detail for most purposes and they should be the currency of reporting beyond the school, including to moderating groups.

The SEAC letter says that teachers will assess children against each attainment target during the Spring Term of the final year of a Key Stage. If the letter means what it appears to say, the accumulation of continuous assessments proposed by TGAT will have no place in the reporting system. This duplication of effort will surely take more teacher-time than the moderation system which TGAT proposed and will lead to a concentration of assessment in one term that will have to take account of work done over 2 or 3 years for Key Stage 1 and 4 years for Key Stage 2: memorizing will have an unduly prominent place. The distortion of work in the final years of the Key Stages will be considerable, and it would be very surprising if teachers were able to keep the curriculum as a whole in mind when dealing in both Spring and Summer terms with the details of assessment required. It is rather as though the car salesman insisted on being paid the price of a car in pound coins because pounds are the basic unit of currency. In at least some cases the assessments settled in the penultimate term of the Key Stage will not actually be used. Where work in an attainment target is assessed in a SAT (it is not yet clear whether every attainment target will be included in a collection of SATs, though it is difficult to think why anyone should even contemplate the possibility), the result will replace the teachers' assessment unless the difference between the two is such that there is 'a change to a profile component result that the teacher wishes to query.' In effect, the moderating system is reduced to an appeals system and there is a tentative proposal that the number of appeals might be reduced by the intervention of a visiting moderator.

The consequences are that the SATS must be much more tightly controlled; that they are presumed to be and to continue to be satisfactory; and the in-service training element of the procedure virtually disappears and with it one of the main ways in which the National Curriculum might have aided improvement in the educational system.

The Nature of Profile Components

The TGAT notion of a profile component had a number of important facets. It grew from a view about the degree of precision that could be expected of a national assessment system, and the complexity of the information that could be handled either by parents or by the education system. It also called for a view about what aspects of learning could be grouped together in such a way as to make sense: as an extreme case, is it possible to give a child a single mark that describes achievement in both the high jump and long multiplication? The profile components were intended to be the biggest groups of aspects of achievement that could reasonably be combined. TGAT also assumed that profile components would change from one level to another not only within subjects but in their relation to subjects and attainment targets.

The SEAC letter acknowledges the difficulties of precision. It considers that reporting in relation to schools and regions 'will best be served by means of profile component and whole subject scores only. To report at any further level of refinement, such as at attainment target level, will tend to overburden the system and is unlikely to be useful.' Elsewhere: 'It would in particular be undesirable to establish aggregation processes of a complexity and sophistication not justified by the accuracy, reliability and validity of the raw data.' Hear! Hear!

Part of SEAC's problem arises from, for example, the English

Statutory Orders' failure to use profile components in anything like the original TGAT sense. The Statutory Orders, prompted it must be said by the English Working Group's report, combine writing for meaning, handwriting and spelling as one profile component. The implication is that ability in one is associated with ability in the other two. Budding authors had better make sure that their handwriting is up to scratch, for otherwise they may be judged as unable to write what they mean. Well, it certainly happens that teachers and others mark down some interesting pieces of writing because they are difficult to read, but the association is not to be encouraged.

Combining assessments of achievement in two or more attainment targets within a profile component is a matter of judgement. Some Working Parties have proposed ways in which the combinations should be managed. The three just mentioned in English are given the weightings of 70:20:10. Even supposing the combination made sense, this seduction by numbers is likely to produce illegitimate offspring. It is after all only necessary to do well at *writing for meaning*, for *handwriting* and *spelling* not to matter with regard to achieving the next level in the profile component. That would be a wrong message to convey to children about spelling and handwriting. Even when attainment targets are equally weighted, there may be curious results if SEAC insists on its present line. Where there are five equally weighted attainment targets in a profile component, a child may achieve Level 6, say, in three of them and still be within Level 1 in the other two and yet be judged to be at Level 6 in the profile component. That is the kind of curiosity that moderating groups could have dealt with given general guidance by SEAC rather than the tight insistence on formulas.

The fact is that it is impossible to produce sensible assessments unless you trust teachers. SEAC could set up a multiple of bureaucratic constraints but the more it seeks precision the more cumbersome the procedure becomes, the less comprehensible it becomes to those who wish to use the results, and the less the results will give a picture of what schools and children are actually doing. In my view, the proposals in the July letter already go beyond what is sensible. They are deficient mainly because of their failure to grasp the advantages of a proper moderating system. They also make too much of the attainment targets when they require information about each attainment target for each child to be handed in to moderating groups, presumably so that something is done with the information: the cost of making sense of the millions of bits of information should be set against the cost of the TGAT moderating system, part of which could properly be regarded as attributable to the in-service training budget.

The Isolation of Subject Working Party Proposals

There are other consequences to the line that is being taken. If each attainment target is treated separately as described in SEAC's July letter, the chance of bringing together compatible attainment targets from different subjects will be diminished if not lost. If, however, SEAC were to grasp the nettle and undertake the re-alignment of subject profile components or even attainment targets within cross-subject profile components, then there would be a good chance of making the assessment load tolerable for primary school teachers.

For example, the use of computers is referred to in relation to a number of subjects and could be considered together. There are many other examples, but two will illustrate the point. In Science Attainment Target 1, Level 2, children are expected to be able to identify simple differences, for example, hot/cold, rough/smooth; in Mathematics Attainment Target 12 Level 2 they are expected to be able to choose criteria to sort and classify objects. Those are essentially the same requirements and could be treated so in the assessment system. In Science Attainment Target 1, Level 5, children are expected to use concepts, knowledge and skills to suggest simple questions and design investigations to answer them; in Mathematics Attainment Target 12, Level 5, they are expected to design and use an observation sheet to collect data; collate and analyze results. For both teaching and assessment purposes, identifying and uniting the overlaps will simplify the task of teachers and assessors. What is required at the national assessment level is that the School Examinations and Assessment Council draws up, certainly for the first two key stages, a shorter, overall list of profile components that will be the basis of assessment, and therefore of SATS at the ends of those stages. It is difficult to say with certainty what they might be when the whole range of Statutory Orders is in place, but a first working list should probably be similar to the following:

Possible profile components

End of key stage 1

1. Communication through the spoken word;
2. Communication through written material
   a. reading
   b. writing
3. Knowledge and application regarding numerical mathematics, including algebra;
4. Physical competence:
   a. fine motor skills
         including the presentation of data, through
         handwriting, number, graphs, diagrams and the
         use of tools and instruments;
   b. gross motor skills
5. The exploration and investigation of physical phenomena, involving measurement and spatial mathematics;
6. The observation and investigation of plants and animals;
7. Personal and social competence;[4]
8. Creative expression and appreciation of the arts;
9. Designing and making;

End of key stage 2

1. Communication through the spoken word;
2. Communication through written material
   a. reading
   b. writing
3. Knowledge and application regarding numerical mathematics, including algebra;

4. Physical competence:
   a. fine motor skills
      including the presentation of data through handwriting, number, graphs, diagrams and the use of tools and instruments;
   b. gross motor skills
5. The exploration and investigation of physical phenomena (including materials, forces, weather, the Earth's physical features), including their location and distribution and involving measurement and spatial mathematics;
6. The observation and investigation of living things;
7. Personal and social competence;
8. Investigation, knowledge and its use concerning past and present societies and their achievements;
9. Creative expression and application of the arts;
10. Designing and making;

Item 7 at keystage 1 has been split into items 7 and 8 in keystage 2.

Reformulating the profile components in this way, or something like it, would have the treble advantage of easing the assessment burden on primary school teachers; of making more sense of the link between teaching and assessment in primary schools; and of being reasonably comprehensible to parents, highlighting things they want to know. The wish of SEAC to report down to the level of attainment targets is, at least in part, probably due to a recognition that highly specific information is sometimes important about an individual child. There is no reason why teachers should not, if reporting according to the framework suggested here, pick up points of particular interest. For example, under 'Creative expression and the appreciation of the arts' it might be right to draw attention particularly to a child's interest and ability in music and, under 'fine motor skills', his or her competence in playing the violin. It is unnecessary to expect teachers of 7-year-olds to provide information *automatically* — either to parents or for recording and reporting purposes — about every child's ability to play musical instruments.

Should there be a Level 0?

There are some indications that SEAC may be thinking that children do not enter Level 1 until they have satisfied the statements of attainment for Level 1. That would be contrary to TGAT's advice that all children should be regarded as working in Level 1 on entry to school and, as they show that they can work at the level of the statements of attainment for Level 1, they should begin moving towards Level 2. I believe that the change from TGAT's view would be a serious disadvantage. All children bring something with them to school and we should not fall into the error of seeming to say that they do not. Expectations and assumptions need to be heightened, not reduced. If children are regarded as being unclassified, or blank, or at Level 0, the urge to assess them intensively so that they may enter (the new) Level 1 will pressurise teachers into unbalanced practices in which assessment will become more important than teaching. Furthermore, the position of children with special needs will be made much worse and could continue in 0 for two, three or more years.

Identifying Progress

The SEAC letter refers to the difficulties of interpreting the results of assessment, especially in their publication. It is widely accepted that the results will be a reflection, though not entirely so, of the nature of the catchment area served by the school. The fear is that schools will be unfairly judged, either being blamed for relatively poor results that are actually just what might be expected or even good for the area, or praised when the nature of the catchment area would suggest that the results should actually be better. There has been a growing view in some quarters that a fairer system would be to report progress made instead of reporting the achievements actually made by children. SEAC expresses an interest in the idea, notes that information on progress would not be available at the end of Key Stage 1, and promises to 'offer guidance to set alongside [the Secretary of State's] encouragement' to schools to publish these results on a voluntary basis.

The belief that schools can best be compared by comparing the progress of their pupils has been encouraged by the work done in connection with *School Matters*,[5] *The School Effect*[6] and a book on ILEA secondary schools by Harvey Goldstein and Desmond Nuttall which was the subject of an article in *Education Guardian*.[7] It was made clear in the last that the statistical techniques used 'suggest strongly that schools cannot be ordered along a single dimension. Schools differ in a number of respects and have different effects on different kinds of children.' In *The School Effect*, it was found that similar children, sometimes sub-groups of similar children, made relatively better progress in some schools than in others where, in absolute terms, higher examination grades were achieved. It also found 'that children belonging to the higher social classes pass far more exams than those belonging to the lower social classes, and also achieve far higher scores in the second year tests. There is also a fairly strong tendency for children from the higher social classes to get better exam results after taking account of the second year test scores.' That is, they make more progress, on average — presumably because the circumstances that have led to their beginning with an advantage continue to have that effect throughout their schooling.

That being so, the publication of the results of progress made will not eliminate differences due to catchment area. Even if it did, what might the consequences be? The results of actual achievement give some clue about the needs of the individual school. Perhaps the children need the help of a teacher skilled in helping those for whom English is a second language, or assistance from the remedial service, or a more generous staffing ratio. If they are then shown to make as much or even more progress than children (of higher absolute attainment) in the school in the affluent area, should those additional resources be withdrawn or even transferred?

There may be some advantage in providing information about progress as well as about levels of achievement, and TGAT itself referred to the possibility in the later stages, but it has to be recognized that the complexity of the information would be increased. There may also be increased pressure to assess/test children on entry to school so that progress could be judged in the first Key Stage. Teachers who objected to 7 as too early for formal assessment would surely and properly object to 5. And if 5, why not 4 or 3?

The move towards supplementing information about levels of achievement with information about progress may arise partly because more precision is expected of the assessment system than it is capable of providing. The whole process as envisaged by TGAT would be more consistent from school to school than what happened previously, but neither it nor anything likely to be practical will provide indisputable evidence about which school is best for a child, or do more than provide pointers about the effectiveness of individual schools to be followed up by more substantial studies. Parents and others will need help if they are to understand the limits of the information they can be given and how to use it in conjunction with other knowledge, gained from visits to schools and accounts of the range of facilities and activities available. They will continue to listen to local opinion of other parents and their children and notice accounts of the school's activities in the local press.

The Effects of Publishing Results

If, as some believe, the catchment area of a school can be categorized by a few good indicators — for example the percentage of pupils qualifying for free meals — then it should be possible for SEAC to provide information about the national distributions of pupils in schools with similar backgrounds. That might be the kind of information to be included in a school brochure against which the distributions of its own pupils could be seen. Whether it is wise to attempt to achieve such doubtful accuracy is not certain. It is still difficult to predict what the consequences will be of publishing results, whether in the TGAT form, or of progress or of both. Many parents living in small communities have no practical choice of primary school. Even in towns, the distance that the buggy has to be pushed may be a deciding factor. Children are already in schools and it is a considerable upheaval to withdraw them and to send them elsewhere, away from their street-mates. Once one child is in a primary school, life is complicated if a second child has to be taken to a different school. Local information has always existed about schools and individual teachers, sometimes well based and sometimes not. At least the system of reporting the numbers of children at each level will make it possible to show that some children in a school do reach high standards, though the proportions will be different in different schools.

Maybe this is a time to hold one's nerve, to increase efforts to inform parents and prospective parents about what is happening in the school, so that when results are published they can be put into a context of prior knowledge.

Undoubtedly SEAC and LEAs should give considerable attention to ways of putting a school's results in context in the other sense. Perhaps information can be collected about each school which will give some indication of the social composition of the neighbourhood and the results of all schools in similar areas be provided for comparison. But it is important to guard against the view that we should be satisfied that children from materially poor homes, or some ethnic minority groups will always do badly. Where the results in schools that cater for them do show up badly then we should be asking ourselves what material provision and what changes of teaching practice we should be making to improve the children's achievements.

Notes

1. DES/WO (1988) *National Curriculum, Task Group on Assessment and Testing: a Report*, London, HMSO.
    DES/WO (1988) *Task Group on Assessment and Testing Report, A Digest for Schools*, reports of committee chaired by Paul Black, London, HMSO.
2. DES (1988) Press Notice 179/88, London, DES.
3. Halsey, P. H. (1989): Letter dated 13th July from the Chairman and Chief Executive of the School Examinations and Assessment Council to the Secretary of State, reference MRF/PUB6/1.
4. These would include assessments of children's ability to work and play in a class/school community, their relations with others, their sense of self and their ability to choose, use and share resources, i.e. one aspect

of the earliest stage of geography and history if those subjects are given a suitably broad interpretation.

5. Mortimer, P., Sammons, P., Stoll, L., Lewis, D. and Ecob, R. (1988) *School Matters: The Junior Years*, Wells, Open Book Publishers.
6. Smith, D. and Tomlinson, S. (1989) *The School Effect: A Study of Multi-Racial Comprehensives*, London, Policy Studies Institute.
7. Goldstein, H. and Nuttall, D. (4 July 1989) *Education Guardian: Screen Tests for Progress*, London, Guardian Newspapers.

Chapter 9

Operating the Curriculum

The teaching of the curriculum depends upon a number of things. There is a range of methodologies from which teachers can choose. In practice the choice is affected by the material resources available, by the nature of the premises, by the support and training provided initially and in-service, part of which may come from colleagues in the school, part from the advisory services and part from the training system. The provision of resources, buildings, in-service training arrangements and the support services and the supply of teachers and ancillary services, depends on the LEA and the Government and, with the introduction of the local management of schools, the governing body.

This chapter concentrates on teaching techniques, timing and school organization.

Teaching Techniques and Style

The Organization of the Children

A glance at the photographs in the Plowden Report shows that teachers in the first half of the 1960s were arranging the children within a class in a variety of ways for teaching purposes. Most of the photographs of children at work show them working alone, in pairs or larger groups. In a number, enough can be seen to show that the whole class is probably engaged in much the same kind of activity: physical education in the playground or hall, using materials to make puppets, making models or music, looking closely at natural phenomena. The only photograph of a class sitting quietly in four rows all facing the same way dates from 1937, though there certainly were similarly arranged classes in the 1960s and I have been in one in England in the second half of the 1980s. In virtually every classroom contemporary with the Plowden Report there would have been, as there still are, times when all of the children sit facing in the same direction engaged in the same activity, for example to listen to the teacher or one of their number telling a story, singing or otherwise making music, making plans of action or drawing together the threads of some relevant experience. There are times when the whole school takes part in the same activity: when the whole school assembles, on sports day, for a drama or poetry festival or, though not in the same space, when a common theme is adopted throughout the school for a week or longer. Of course, individual children make different contributions to, and take different things from, the same activity, whether they are working in a pair or as a member of the whole school community.

The trend towards recognizing individual differences between children undoubtedly led to a sense that children should be given individual and separate tasks at least in some of their work. There is still a universal opinion among primary school teachers as well as among parents that the teaching of reading, writing and mathematics is highly important, as it is. Small improvements in performance seem easier to identify in reading and mathematics than in most other things — though they are not quite so easy as they seem. The two aspects of learning at which children most often work individually on graded material are reading and mathematics.

In fact, there is no good reason why the recognition of individual differences and the provision of individual work should be tied together in a detailed and absolute way. The selection of tasks and the teaching and learning associated with them depend on other factors than small steps in progress alone. Furthermore, the ability to work together, to cooperate, is an important attribute and depends on a set of skills that schools should help children towards acquiring. Teaching each child in a class separately, except occasionally and for specific purposes, is not within the capacity of most human beings. All too often the attempt to do so, even in mathematics, has led to the teacher creating a mass of individual pathways — sets of cards, text books and so on — which children move through with little stimulus from others. Even the teacher's interventions are mainly concerned with guiding the child to the materials. The tendency towards this kind of individual working in mathematics was noticed in the 1978 HMI survey[1] and in the ORACLE research,[2] even where the classroom furniture was arranged in such a way as to suggest that children worked in groups.

There are, in my experience, real dangers in dividing work *as a matter of routine* into small progressive steps which children take individually. One is that children can find it difficult to see the wood for the trees, for their attention is focused on such small steps. Another is that the teacher is called upon to go over the same ground at short intervals as one child after another comes up against the same difficulties during the course of a week or two. Drawing together children who are at about the same stage in an aspect of their learning can save teaching time; and if children are encouraged to work together in acquiring the skill or idea, then they can profitably learn from each other. In practice, the claim is not born out that individual work allows children to make continuous progress. What happens is that the material, whether reading books or mathematics work cards, is stepped and the children soon find themselves caught within a step and find it difficult to catch the teacher's attention for long enough to show that they could proceed. A system that seems to be capable of sustaining a close match between the child's capacity and the work done proves to be impossible to operate in practice, as was shown by Neville Bennett and Charles Desforges in their study on match.[3] They, unlike the 1978 HMI survey, found that the work of the lower achievers was often pitched too high. That is what common sense suggests, and I was surprised by the evidence in the HMI survey which indicated that where the match for such children was poor it was more likely to be due to underexpectation, but the evidence was reported as found. What is incontestable is that children working near to the limit of their capacities are more likely to need their teacher's attention than will those who are coasting along. Children who can do more and who know more are often less demanding simply because they are working well within their limits.

We ought to be trying to spread the demands we make more evenly across the children being taught, to recognize that the match between the teaching provided and each child's learning needs cannot be exact, and to accept grouping in mathematics that brings together children who, for the present, need much the same teaching.

Worries that individual work in mathematics has become too extensive were supported by the findings of the ORACLE research. When Maurice Galton and his team compared achievement in basic skills according to the general style of teaching used, they found little consistent difference one to another. I shall discuss the styles later in this chapter. What is of interest now is that they identified common characteristics of the more successful teachers in three of the styles and found that those teachers did not spend much of their time in short interactions with the children to ensure, mainly, that they were getting on with the task in hand. They did give clear instructions to start with, mainly to a group or the class; they were able to discuss underlying ideas and general issues related to the task and asked more open-ended questions — what the team calls higher order interactions; they encouraged children to seek out the answers to problems; but they also gave regular feedback about the way the work was going. From the point of view of the individual child, membership of a group made it possible to engage in more sustained interactions with the teacher. Much the same points have been made again more recently in *The Teaching and Learning of Mathematics* by HMI.[4] While reporting some improvement in the teaching of mathematics and a 1.5 per cent improvement in the performance of 11-year-olds, HMI still found, as in the 1978 Survey, that a stress on providing children with individual assignments led to there being 'too few occasions of direct teaching to the whole class or a particular group in order to consolidate the children's grasp of important mathematical principles . . . '

None of that is to say that children should never work individually in mathematics. Where a child is showing that he or she has specific difficulties, then there is an obvious case for specific action and individual discussion and practice. All children need individual practice from time to time, and the chance to work through a problem and come to terms with its implications. These activities also require the teacher's attention and time, and quiet discussion with the child. These are not easy to arrange in a classroom where there is one teacher who has little or no time free from class responsibility. It is easy to say, though more difficult to arrange, that some times can be found during a week when most of the children are engaged on routine things, working within the limits of their skills but applying them to some larger purpose, for example arranging information they have collected. The younger the children the more difficult that is to do, and especially so when most of the children are not yet independent readers.

There is a different issue that has to be kept in mind in teaching children to read. The argument there does call for more individual engagement, though reading in pairs and threes can be useful, as can encouraging a group of children to read the same book separately and then produce a joint oral or written review. A danger in the teaching of reading is that too much time is spent with children reading aloud. Of course some is necessary so that the teacher may try to discover whether the child is finding difficulties which require teaching action, but not so often to check which page the child is at. It is also useful for children to have the experience of reading to groups or the whole school for specific purposes. But too much reading aloud can slow the whole process down, make it more difficult for children to make sense of what they are reading and to use the sense to enable them to interpret more of what is written.

Sometimes the reason for dividing the children into groups and possibly having some working individually is to make the best use of the space. Another obvious use of grouping is to make the best use of resources, human and material. A group may be formed to work with an incoming teacher, whether that be with someone specially employed to work with children whose first language is not English (or Welsh in some Welsh schools), or to work with a group of children with special educational needs. Infant class teachers for many years and junior class teachers for fewer have arranged a number of distinct working areas for their classes, each equipped with the tools, instruments and materials necessary for what is to be done in them. Division of the children into subgroups is one reason why teaching spaces today are equipped with a much richer variety of materials and equipment than was the case in the 1950s. If everything the children use has to be bought in multiples of 30, both the cost and the storage problem would allow a far narrower range.

Working in groups ought also to be a positive curricular activity, not simply a matter of organizational convenience. During their years in a primary school, children should be learning to work alone, in groups of different sizes, and as a member of a group that is itself contributing to the work of a still larger group, even the whole school. When a school adopts a unifying theme for a period and each child and class contributes, it is important to make the experience explicit by discussing its implications with the children and drawing parallels with the ways groups outside schools operate.

From time to time children need to occupy different positions in the group, and the groups themselves need to be composed according to different criteria. For example, a group may be formed to carry out a task that, because of its magnitude, would be beyond any one member, though each contributes much the same skills and effort; the group may or may not need a leader, and children should have the chance of acting as leaders and as led and understanding the subtleties of those roles so that they do not suppose that a leader must be dictatorial or that the led have no say in the purposes of the group and methods used. Children should sometimes be members of groups in which each contributes a different skill or capacity. At least some children should, by the end of the primary school stage, be ready to think about the kind of group that needs to be formed from the people available if it is to do a particular job well.

Sometimes, as was suggested earlier in reference to the teaching of mathematics, it is sensible to form a group because its members need the same teaching and practice. Sometimes mixed ability groups are better because even the more able members learn from formulating explanations. Quite apart from the content and skills being explored, children should be brought to regard helping others as a proper and worthwhile activity. It is not sensible to form a group according to one criterion, for example the children's ability in mathematics, and to keep the group in being for all purposes or for the whole year.

As with so many aspects of teaching, there is no simple and universal answer to the question: which is best, individual work, group work or class work? The purpose and content is all important. The factors that have to be taken into account in deciding may even pull in different directions. They certainly include the teacher's capacity to reach a clear understanding with the children about what is to be done; his or her capacity to keep an eye and ear on more than one thing at a time; and to bring out the underlying principles in what is being learnt. They include the total number of children involved and the amount and type of space and materials available. They certainly include the nature of the teaching and learning that is sought, and the maturity, capacities and even the moods of the children.

In short, a registration group may be broken down into groups to improve the match between the work being done and the children's learning needs; to provide opportunities for the children to be taught to work in groups of various kinds and play various roles within them; to make the best of the teachers' time and the resources available; to allow access to a wider range of materials and equipment than would otherwise be possible in the space and with the funds provided. Individual work has a place, but much more time is usefully spent with children working in twos or larger groups, though not every group member may make precisely the same contribution to what is done or get the same from the experience. As with all forms of organization, the organization is best chosen to suit an end, none is better in principle than any other, though the organization should be as simple as will allow the purposes to be achieved.

Teachers today are better able to manage these complexities of organization than used to be the case. The danger has been that individualization has sometimes seemed a goal in itself rather than one of a number of possible means to an end: the enhancement of children's learning.

The Timing of Activities

It was still possible for a decade or more after 1944 to find master timetables in some primary schools, framed behind glass, and signed by a pre-war HMI, as was then required. In the end they were kept as curios. They rarely fitted the number of classes in the school and did not correspond to what was being done. In most secondary schools, the production of the annual timetable is still a major event. The inclination and disadvantages have already been noted of regarding the timetable as synonymous with the curriculum. What are they actually for? Well, at root, to make sure that the children, the teachers and the necessary space, equipment and apparatus get together so that teaching and learning can go on. If expertise is parcelled out among the staff and some of the equipment and apparatus is tied to particular parts of the premises, then the timetable apportions what is available so that each pupil gets an appropriate share. Where there are a lot of pupils and there is a lot of parcelling out, the process of allocating space, time and expertise for all the children in a school gets complicated. No one could face making wholly new and complex timetables weekly, though some changes have to be made to meet unexpected events, like staff absences. In general what is put into operation at the beginning of a school year remains in force for the rest of it.

If the resources are all available at arms reach, and the teacher is able to deal with all the educational needs of the 30 or so children for whom he or she is responsible, then there is no need to draw up a fixed school-timetable to be held to for the whole year. It is useful to have some general plan for the distribution of time, at least so that some things will surely be done. They do not have to be done on the same day each week or the same time of each day. They may not be done for the same amount of time each week. During a week, the actual time allocation might be different for different groups of children within the same class. With one teacher and using readily available resources, it is possible to adapt to the children's educational needs in a much more complex way than can be managed through an annual school-timetable. What matters is that the children are getting a broad and balanced curriculum: in the terms of the earlier discussions on the curriculum, assessment and children's characteristics, that they are making progress across a range of skills, ideas and so on. On the other hand there is disadvantage in chopping about without reason, and a degree of regularity helps everyone to know where they are.

The differences in the kinds of complexity involved are that the total secondary school timetable is a complex system to produce and modify but relatively simple for the individual teacher to operate, whereas the primary school arrangement even as described so far is complex to operate.

Within the registration group it is and always has been universal or almost universal for the whole group to engage together in physical education, when listening to a story or taking a broadcast programme and for music except when working with a peripatetic teacher. The same applies to religious education, especially when taking part in the school assembly. These activities take up a significant part of each week and should not be forgotten when people talk about individual work or mixing activities. Some teachers, an increasing number as the children get older, arrange that the whole class works on the same aspect of the curriculum together, and may do so in such a way that the pattern of work is repeated each week. Often, mathematics takes up part of the morning, and the 1987 DES Primary School Staffing Survey indicated that the subject took up about a quarter of school time altogether. There has been a tendency for work that might be specifically labelled as English also to be given time in the mornings, including listening to children read books specifically designed to extend their reading, and writing other than that concerned with historical/geographical/scientific topics. Art, crafts, topic work often occupy the afternoons. Physical education and music, because of the relative shortage of space and specialist requirements, may take place throughout the day.

Such arrangements are usually justified on two grounds. First, it is easier for the teacher to keep track if the children are working on much the same thing, though not necessarily at precisely the same level. The ILEA report, *School Matters*[5] concluded, so far as junior age classes are concerned, that that was a significant factor in producing effective teaching. The other relates to the concentration on the 'basics' in the morning. The argument is that children are more alert in the morning, so the more important things must be done then. I have three doubts about the second justification. The first arises from the acknowledged fact that adults are not all at their best in the morning, some are more alert later in the day: I know of no reason to suppose that children are all the same in this respect. The second is from watching children in the Pioneer Palaces in the Soviet Union taking on far more demanding activities — in mathematics and technology as well as in more artistic activities — in the afternoons and early evenings as compared with what they had been doing at school in the morning. The third is the most important. The concentration on the 'basics' in the morning has led to missed opportunities to learn and extend learning in English and mathematics through applying knowledge in topic work and otherwise, whenever it is done.

In many classes for infants and some for older children, teachers prefer to arrange at least some of the work so that children in the class are engaged on different aspects of the curriculum at the same time. The doubts of the authors of the ILEA report have already been mentioned. Nevertheless, some teachers find that they can use their own time more effectively with their pupils if some are engaged on activities that occupy them without requiring frequent help from the teacher. The system is undoubtedly more complex to operate and some arrangement is necessary to enable the teacher to keep an eye on what has been and is being done. Some teachers permit choice to be made from a small number of activities, or allocate children to them to begin with and then allow change. An arrangement may be made so that children's work is deposited in different boxes according to curricular aspect, or children sign on a wallsheet when the teacher signals that what they have done is satisfactory.

Teacher Typologies, Organization and Timing

The various teacher-typologies that have been constructed have attempted to cluster together aspects of teachers' practices. The simple division between formal and informal continues to cause interest, though, as the work of Gray and Satterley[6] indicates, the dichotomy is too crude to be a useful one in the study of teacher effectiveness. The ORACLE typology, mentioned earlier, identified four main styles, with the fourth subdivided into three. Briefly, they are as follows:

Style 1: just over 1 in 5 teachers arranged for the children to work individually — though even for these only about 30 per cent of time was spent on individual work. When it was, there was a concentration on task supervision, so that exchanges between pupils and teachers were frequent, short and low level, for example giving permission to go on to the next exercise or providing a correct spelling. The teacher may sit at his or her desk, to which the children come for help, or move about among them. They were referred to as *individual monitors.*

Style 2: this was used by about 1 teacher in 7. These teachers engaged in a substantial amount of class teaching. They used many open and closed questions and made more statements of ideas and problems than other teachers. They were designated *class directed enquirers.*

Style 3: made up about an eighth of the teachers seen. Their interaction with groups of pupils was about three times greater than that of other styles. They were more concerned with statements of fact than Style 2 teachers, but did make more than average use of open questions. They were called *group instructors.*

Style 4: accounted for about a half of the teachers. To some extent these used a mixture of the other styles. Some of these teachers made *infrequent changes* from one style to another, some made *frequent changes* and some *rotated* pupils from one activity to another at regular intervals. The actions of the last sub-group carry the serious disadvantage that the time-spans allowed cannot possibly be suited to all of the children and to all of the activities. At least when the whole class changes together from one common activity to another some account can be taken of the inherent requirements of an activity. The research found that children in classes run by *rotational changers* generally had considerable problems in improving the level of their achievement in basic skills.

As has already been indicated, the same researchers found it possible to identify successful teachers representing different styles.

Perhaps what is to be learnt from the attempts to categorize teachers is that there is little to be gained from producing such typologies. There are aspects of learning that benefit from specific teaching approaches, there are children whose personalities and backgrounds lead them to respond better to some forms of approach than others, and teachers' own personalities and knowledge make it easier for them to teach in some ways rather than in others. What is needed is that teachers are well acquainted with the range of possibilities and that their initial and in-service training extends the range of their options and helps them to choose approaches and resources with insight. As with so many aspects of education, there is no pot of pure gold at the end of the rainbow.

Inter-class Organization

There are relatively few primary school teachers who have sole and complete charge of their classes and are unaffected by the activities of other teachers. In a school of any size, access to shared resources like the hall or the library or the one television set or microcomputer might have to be sorted out well in advance, and perhaps on a yearly cycle. Where only a half-dozen or so people are involved, then a formal yearly allocation can be changed relatively easily and temporarily by negotiation.

Additional complications occur where more than one teacher is concerned with a class. This happens much more than is commonly supposed, and the 1978 HMI survey[7] found that 85 per cent of 9-year-olds were taught by teachers additional to the class teacher.

The figures were 73 per cent for 7-year-olds and 90 per cent for 11-year-olds. Nearly a third of the 9-year-old classes met at least three other teachers than their own. In just over 40 per cent of classes with 9-year-olds, the amount of time spent with incoming teachers amounted to between 2 and 5 hours a week. In nearly 10 per cent of classes the figure was 5 hours or more. The additional teachers provided for a range of curricular activities, not always with all members of a class. The table for the percentage of classes with 9-year-olds taught by a teacher other than their own class teacher, broken down by subjects, was as follows:

Percentage	Subjects
50	Music
35	Language
30	Physical education
20	Art and Craft
10	Mathematics
5	French
5	Science

The figures are to the nearest 5 per cent.

The incoming teacher may be another full-time or part-time member of the school staff, or someone who works in a number of schools, for example a peripatetic teacher of music or of reading. The number of teachers supporting and sometimes replacing the class teacher has almost certainly increased during the 1980s, partly because Section 11 teachers who work with children with little or no English are not now commonly class teachers, and more Advisory Teachers have been appointed, frequently through the central Government's Educational Support Grants scheme.

There would be no sense in trying to maintain a wholly non-timetabled employment of incoming teachers, whether on the school staff or additional to it. The fact that some pre-planning has to be effected does not mean that it is necessary to go to the extreme of timetabling every activity. Indeed, as much room as possible ought to be left for adjusting the arrangements either for specific and short-lived purposes or because some other allocation of time would be better long-term. The range of provision that has to be allowed for is considerable. In one case three or four 11-year-olds who have been on a nature walk go along to the infant teacher who can best help them to work up their field sketches; in another the curricular leader for mathematics comes in to help a half-dozen children who are moving into the idea of rotational symmetry; in another the visiting advisory teacher visits one (out of a number) for six weeks on Wednesday afternoons; in another case, the violin teacher calls year after year on Thursdays or the leading school musician takes a class at regular intervals throughout the year. There is no need to cast all teacher movement in concrete because some must be.

Some witnesses to the House of Commons Select Committee[8] thought that primary school teachers need extra support in some aspects of the curriculum, and they favoured a system whereby members of staff took on the job of advising others in one or more curricular fields. Some also thought that such a teacher, acting as a coordinator, should undertake direct teaching of children in other classes only if working alongside their teacher. This has seldom happened in the teaching of children having difficulty in learning to read, nor is it common with music. The witnesses' worry was that the advantages that accrue from having one teacher responsible for the work of a class would be lost.

The advantages of the class: teacher system arise from the fact that the teacher and children are together for a long time and get to know each other in a variety of teaching and learning circumstances. One aspect of a child's learning can be brought in to help and fill out another. It is possible to adapt to immediate needs without consulting many other teachers.

However, the curricular demands on teachers have increased greatly in the last thirty years, and it is too much to expect any one teacher to deal with the curriculum unaided. Some of the support can be provided outside the children's hours, but sometimes help is needed directly with teaching. If some of that is to come from other members of the school staff, then it is inevitable that there will be times when children will not be in contact with their own teacher. Classes also have to be taught without their class teacher's presence if that teacher is to have non-contact time for preparation, consultation with other teachers, parents, medical and social workers during the school day, as well as for record keeping and assessment purposes. The problem is one of balancing advantages. In my view it would be very disadvantageous to go anywhere near as far as the traditional secondary school system of specialization, especially because one of the strengths of primary schools has been that children and teachers do get to know each other well. It is also an inescapable fact that this closeness and length of contact is unhelpful in some circumstances for some children and some teachers, but the advantages for the overwhelming majority outweigh the disadvantages for the relatively few, whose needs should be treated specifically.

Some part-way house is needed to reduce the problems that come from one person trying to deal with all the children across the whole curriculum. There are two limiters to how far primary school children should come into contact with more than one teacher. The first is that no change of teacher should occur for change's sake. The incoming teacher should undertake work with the children that their own teacher cannot provide, even with prior advice. The second is that the class teacher should be in overall charge of the class, orchestrating the actual work that is done by the incoming teachers and linking it together for the children involved so that the whole makes sense to them. If those conditions apply, then I am not especially concerned with the geographical location of the work, it might take place inside the home classroom alongside the class teacher or not, or it might take place outside the home classroom. The essential requirement is that it contributes to a coherent school experience for the children.

The form of organization requires the headteacher and each member of staff to concern themselves with the school as a whole, with individuals, from time to time taking special responsibility for an aspect of the curriculum and/or a class or sub-group of children. It has been called 'collegial', and as Robin Alexander has pointed out[9] may not appeal to all class teachers, let alone all headteachers, for it calls for the acceptance of wider responsibilities than systems that are relatively paternalistic/maternalistic, Unfortunately, the other options are either a movement towards a more intensive specialization such as is found in many secondary schools, or a simplification of the curriculum which is not in keeping with the National Curriculum and, far more important, is not in keeping with the capacities and needs of the children or of society at large.

Notes

1. DES/HMI (1978) *Primary Schools in England*, paragraph 5.65, London, HMSO.
2. Simon, B. (1980) *Inside the Primary Classroom*, 22, 3, pp. 68ff., *Forum*, Leicester, PSW (Educational) Publications.
3. Bennett, N. and Desforges, C. (1984) *Quality of Pupil Learning Experiences*, Hove, Erlbaum (Lawrence) Associates Ltd.
4. DES/HMI (1989) *Aspects of Primary Education, The Teaching and Learning of Mathematics*, London, HMSO.
5. Mortimer, P., Sammons, P., Stoll, L., Lewis, D. and Ecob, R. (1988) *School Matters: The Junior Years*, p. 253, Wells, Open Book Publishers.
6. Gray, J., Satterley, D. (1981) *Formal or Informal? A reassessment of the British evidence* 51, 2, pp. 190–193, British Journal of Educational Psychology.
7. DES/HMI (1978) *Primary Education in England*, p. 33, London, HMSO.
8. House of Commons Education, Science and Arts Committee (1986) *Achievement in Primary Schools*, Third Report, Session 1985–86, HC 40–I, London, HMSO.
9. Alexander, R. J. (1984) *Primary Teaching*, pp. 180–183, Eastbourne, Holt Education.

Chapter 10

The Beginning of a New Road

A little over twenty years have passed since the Plowden Report was published. That is a short time in educational terms: about three generations of primary school pupils and a half of the potential professional lifetime of a primary school teacher. There have been changes outside the schools in terms of social attitudes, the availability of advanced technical resources, in our perceptions of the children and even in the children themselves. Relatively unusual teaching techniques and organizational arrangements of the mid-1960s have become commonplace. The range of resources has increased significantly, though not necessarily in the volume that is desirable. Primary school teachers, including headteachers, have generally absorbed the changes and improved the service they give to their pupils and to society at large. Now the implementation of the 1988 Education Reform Act heralds more changes, as yet untried in some of their aspects. Much of the National Curriculum will be familiar, though it will call for more to be done in some parts, some schools and some subjects. The 1987 DES Primary School Staffing Survey found that, on average, primary schools spend about 6.5 per cent of their time on science. The Science Subject Working Party reckoned that what it was proposing would require about 12.5 per cent of available time. Many teachers have expressed worries about the teaching of science. Technology has hardly been contemplated by most as yet.

It will be important for everyone to remember in these new times of change what has been achieved in recent decades. The new times are being built on previous achievements, not on disaster, and those in the DES, LEAs, the NCC and SEAC will be wise to listen carefully to what teachers have to say about the opportunities and difficulties associated with the changes. The earlier chapters might have suggested to some readers that primary school teachers have been so concerned with what must be done in schools and with children that they have given too little united thought to the direction in which primary education has been going and, to some extent, had been pushed by external views and circumstances. Teaching children is what is most important, of course, but it will matter more in the future than in the past for primary school teachers to voice their opinions, based on the experience of teaching young children, about changes that are determined from outside, and to do so early in any discussion.

The Pitch of the National Curriculum

Of course it is no use simply trying to swim against the stream. Times change and needs change. The introduction of the National Curriculum is the beginning of a new stage for primary education. The various Subject Working Groups and the NCC and SEAC have worked to tight time-scales. Even if they had had longer, it is highly unlikely that they would have worked out an arrangement that is as much as 80 per cent right for today's circumstances. Today's circumstances, it has to be remembered, encompass the children, the education system including the teachers and the resources available, and the proclivities and requirements of individuals and groups outside the education system. Each of those is itself permanently in a state of change, and so even if the arrangements so far proposed were absolutely right for now, they would become dated and need to be altered in time.

Perhaps the effort that has been put into the construction of the National Curriculum will cause some reduction in the wish for change on the part of politicians and others. Odd though it may seem at present, that will prove to be unfortunate if it leads to a lack of interest and a failure to put money and effort into making and keeping the system as up-to-date and efficient as it should be to meet the needs of the children and society.

There are three advantages that the National Curriculum can bring to teachers. One is that the major demands upon them are public and agreed through Parliament: there are limits as well as requirements. Of course, in this first stage the demands may not be pitched right. They may be too constrained, in which case the public will have to make its voice heard through the politicians. They are more likely to be too extensive, because the briefs that have been given to the Subject Working Parties are that they should work according to the best existing practice. Since they have each been concerned with a major slice of the curriculum, as carved, the presumption is that each school should be expected to be at the level of what is now the best right across the curriculum. No schools in the past have reached such a state of excellence and it seems improbable, schools being the work of people, that any will in future. A few have been good in all aspects of their work and at the highest level in one or two, usually in some classes and not others.

Even if the Government had been content to raise all-round effectiveness to the level of the good, it would still have been necessary to fund the use of some additional resources. Aiming for the best means that additional resources are vital.

Priorities in Improving Resources

The most urgent need, taking primary education as a whole, is for more generous staffing that will provide elbow room so that individual teachers with appropriate knowledge and skills can act as curricular leaders or coordinators either within their own schools or, in the case of small schools or esoteric specialities, across a group of schools. The 1987 DES Primary School Staffing Survey showed that there are 16,400 primary school teachers (out of about 160,000) who have either specialized in mathematics in their initial training course or have had at least a moderately substantial course in teaching mathematics since. There are 22,000 who have done the same in science, probably most of them in the biological sciences. There are over 54,000 with equivalent backgrounds in English, including drama and the teaching of reading; and a handful in technology.

The figures show that there are shortages of expertise in some subjects and it is hardly surprising that they are the same subjects as are proving difficult in secondary schools. There are not enough teachers with more than the basic requirements in mathematics to allow one such teacher per school. Of course, there could not be a teacher with additional qualifications for each subject in every primary school, for most have many fewer teachers than there are Foundation Subjects. There is plainly a need to think of the primary phase as a system and not simply as a number of wholly distinct establishments. Under the new arrangements for the local management of schools that is going to call for considerable activity by LEAs in bringing together headteachers and governing bodies so that they operate within a network, sharing the special knowledge and skills of staff as necessary.

The regrettable fact is that teachers with specialities already in primary schools are prevented from giving the help and guidance they could by the narrow margin between the number of classes and the number of teachers. Including headteachers, there have for many years been about 1.13 teachers per class in primary schools as against about 1.4 in secondary schools. As things were in 1987, the *average* amount of time that Scale 1 and Scale 2 teachers had away from their own classes was 8 minutes per day, many had none.

The roles of curricular coordinators have been discussed elsewhere. Whether for one school or for a group of schools, the job includes giving advice and, when necessary, teaching children in other classes. Giving advice inevitably includes preparing papers for and leading staff discussion. The coordinator has a responsibility for keeping up-to-date with what is happening in other schools in the locality and more widely, and with current research. Even before the recent plethora of documents from the DES, NCC and SEAC, primary school teachers found it very difficult to keep up with the literature across the field. The system of coordinators narrows the range for which any one person is responsible. The fields may not only be the Foundation Subjects. They may also include, as examples, teachniques of assessment and, especially for the head and deputy, issues of school management. It matters for the practical reasons of coverage and for the general health of the system that there are not two kinds of primary school teacher, class teachers and 'specialist' teachers. It is important, as was indicated earlier, that the class teacher should be the orchestrator of the work done by his or her class, no matter who actually teaches it. The class teacher is always likely to be responsible for most of the teaching of a class, even for 11-year-olds, and is in the best position to see that the curriculum makes sense as a whole to the children, and is kept in balance.

None of this is to say teachers need time away from their class only to act as coordinators. They also need some time for preparation that ought to be done when the children are in school; they require time to meet other professionals and parents with whom it may not be possible to speak outside school hours. They must have time to attend courses that are of such substance that they cannot be squeezed into the evenings. They may need time with a few children and will need time to record as they assess children, not only at the ends of the key stages, but throughout the years if parents and the next teachers are to be informed as they should be.

Where Might the Teachers Come From?

The immediate and main solution is probably not to train larger numbers of teachers. It takes a long time to benefit from such a plan. The initial teacher training system has to be geared up and that can usually be done only gradually over some years. There is something like a year's delay before the first extended intake is admitted and either another year or another four years — depending on whether the course is for PGCE or B.Ed. — before the students turn into teachers. There are approximately as many trained teachers not teaching as there are now teaching. The first requirement is to persuade some of them to return.

Some who do return take their first steps as supply teachers, replacing those who are temporarily absent, for whatever reason. Such teachers can be difficult to find. Some practices are being developed by schools and LEAs that should be more encouraging to them. Probably the first requirement is to attempt to keep in touch with teachers when they first leave, to invite them back to functions and to provide specially devised courses that help people not to feel out-of-date. When the teachers are employed for short spells, they should be engaged for a time, whenever possible, that begins just before the regular teachers go off and lasts until just after their return, to allow adequate briefing and de-briefing. Some schools have standard packs of materials — pencils, paper and so on — that the supply teacher can pick up on arrival and so be ready for a businesslike start. Some have information sheets that tell the shape of the school day and explain what to do in the case of emergencies, for example an accident to a pupil. But the need for such good ideas would be reduced if the practice of many heads of keeping an informal attachment with two or three compatible people was formalized. It ought to be recognized that teachers are going to be absent and for each school to be able to set aside a proportion of its budget as a retainer for such teachers who would, in return, guarantee a given number of days work per term.

Specific Teacher Shortages

Three kinds of teacher shortage have been discussed in the preceding paragraphs. They are a shortage of people with special expertise in some parts of the work of schools; the shortage of teachers whose presence would allow those with special expertise to use it with their colleagues; and the shortage of supply teachers. Those apply to virtually all primary schools in England and Wales. There are two other kinds of shortage. The one most publicised is the shortage of teachers in some localities, notably but by no means only, the Home Counties and parts of Inner London. The other is the shortage of teachers trained to work with under-5s.

Perhaps I should add that the word 'shortage' is being used in this chapter to refer to the difference between the numbers of teachers in post and the number needed to do the work that is expected of them. The DES use the word to refer to the smaller difference between the number of teachers and the number of posts currently established.

Ancillary Workers

An increase in the numbers of ancillary workers, especially in areas where many children speak English as a second language, could help free teachers to concentrate more on aspects of their work that are closer to the essence of teaching: assessing their pupils' present capabilities and encouraging, guiding and directing them in increasing their capabilities. If they are to play a full part, the ancillary workers also need some training, including in-service training, even when they have had the advantage of initial training under the Nursery Nurses Examination Board's regulations. It would be naive to try to devise a replacement formula that proposes that x teachers equals y ancillary workers, though it might be worth conducting action research to consider how many ancillary workers (I assume that it would be less than one) should support each teacher. Account needs to be taken of the demands that ancillary workers make on teachers' time.

Material Resources

I have concentrated on the need for people to carry out the National Curriculum. There is also a need for improvement in the equipping of schools. The most obvious call is for more microcomputers, and it is sad that the National Curriculum Technology Working Group seems to have made no adequate case for an increase.

Towards a Staffing Policy

Counting the Work to be Done

It would be wholly unrealistic to expect all that is missing to be provided overnight even if the new roles for primary school teachers could be adopted without time and training for them. What is required is the development of a hard-headed and convincing argument that relates resourcing to the demands on the service. It is no help to go on making a simple plea for smaller registration classes. LEAs have developed activity-led staffing models for secondary schools. The early steps that have been taken in developing such models for primary schools need to be taken further. The start has to be a description of the work that must be done in a primary school. Now that the National Curriculum is in place that should be easier to do. The factors to be taken into account include:

a. the range of teaching to be undertaken;
   this depends on:
   the range of the material to be taught
   the number and range of children to be taught
   the variety of teaching groups that need to be formed
b. the liaison necessary within the school;
   this includes:
   operating the assessment and record system
   the interactions between the teachers so that a
      planned and coherent programme is operated
   the interactions between teachers so that the necessary
      expertise is available
   the interactions between the teaching staff and the
      ancillary staff so that the two groups work in
      concert.
c. the liason necessary with people outside school;
   this includes liaison with:
   parents
   medical and social workers, police
   educational psychologists
   teachers in other schools, especially those from which
      the children come and those to which they go
   the LEA advisory service, including advisory teachers
      community groups, local trades, professions and
      industries
   educational and other suppliers
d. the administrative and management requirements;
   these include:
   work related to the governing body

providing information required by the LEA, DES, NCC and SEAC, and also informing them when it is thought they should be told

keeping staff records, operating the appraisal system

budgetting and accounting

preparing school brochures and other information for parents and others in the community

preparing the working documents for the curriculum, and maintaining the pupils' records

(Note, some of these may properly involve teachers other than headteacher)

e. the number and specialities of the teachers;

this may at first sight seem a surprising inclusion, but of course these two factors affect the likely numbers of absences, the requirement for in-service training, the requirement for 'topping-up' gaps.

The Teacher : Class Ratio

Another simpler approach is to estimate what is required to administer the school as a whole, what is required to administer a class, and what teacher-time is required per class, including support for the class teacher.

Every assumption must be open to challenge and modification, but what follows is one possible series of calculations:

a. assume that the number of classes in a school is determined by dividing the number of children by 30, each 30 and any remainder would count as a class (it should be said that actual schools might choose to divide the children differently);

b. the curriculum is assumed to be a nine subject curriculum (it will be remembered that it does not follow that a school should have a nine subject timetable);

c. each class teacher needs 1 hour support per week in the three core subjects and technology, and 1 hour per fortnight in the remaining subjects except his/her own, i.e. a minimum of 6

arrangements for breaking the registration class into smaller teaching groups from time to time;

d. 1 hour per week per class should be allowed for consultations about individual children with parents, psychologists, school nurse, etc;

e. 2 hours per class plus 5 hours per school (of whatever size) should be allowed for administration.

f. assume a 23.5 hour teaching week.

A school of 200 children would require:

$200 \div 30 = 6 \times 30 +$ a remainder, i.e. 7 classes
$7 \times 23.5 = 164.5$ hours per week basic teaching time
$7 \times 6 = 42$ hours per week support
$7 \times 2 = 14$ hours administration
$7 \times 1 = 7$ hours consultation
$1 \times 5 = 5$ hours school administration
Total $\overline{232.5}$ teaching hours

Since these are all 'in school hours' teaching requirements, the school would then need $(232.5 \div 23.5)$ teachers, i.e. 9.8 full time equivalent teachers.

A similar calculation based on a two-class school leads to a need for 2.9 teachers.

These staffing ratios are very close to the class : teacher staffing ratios of 1 : 1.4 in the lower classes of secondary schools.

They undoubtedly leave some problems, especially for small schools where the number of pupils is closely approaching an exact multiple of 30.

The Need for Further Study

It would be wrong to suppose that the presently agreed formulas for staffing are the last word. They may prove to be clearly unsuitable as the demands on schools change. In the meantime ideas such as those expressed above need to be tested out in representative studies of what teachers do now, and what they have to leave undone. If it cannot be found elsewhere, perhaps some of the money being spent on management training could be used to discover more precisely what the management and teaching loads are. The introduction of plans for funding the local management of schools has led some LEAs to seek ways of improving the funding of their primary schools, and it would be wrong to suppose that a clearly worked out expression of the needs of primary schools would fall on deaf ears either among local and central administrators or politicians. What will not succeed is a simple demand for smaller registration classes.

Improving the Service to the Children

In many ways primary education generally is better now than it was at the time of the Plowden Report, and certainly better than in 1944. Children read and write more widely. They engage with a more extensive range of mathematics. They use class and school libraries in pursuing information and ideas. There has been an increase in the practical applications of mathematics, a development that was being urged as long ago as before the First World War. The variety of teaching provided in art, light crafts, music and physical education has been much extended. There has, in the last decade, been some increase in the teaching and learning of observational and experimental science and some profound if not sufficiently widespread developments in the use of microcomputers and in design and technology. The last two need further extension and topic work needs to be made more coherent through the school so that progression and continuity are improved. There may need to be some increase in briskness, but that will be achieved more effectively by helping children to set their own timescales than by harrassing them. Schools still need to play their part in improving attitudes to race and gender and to consider closely how they can adjust work so that it encourages high achievement in children from homes that doubt whether schools and schooling are really for them.

Where parents have been brought more closely in touch with

what schools do they almost always admire what they see and give support to what is being done.

The next years offer opportunities for still further improvements in the education of young children. The fact that the curriculum and so much else is now more public will make it all the more important for primary school teachers to find a public voice, but the strongest voice of all will come from quality in the classroom. The young teachers I have met in recent years lead me to be optimistic that the voice will be strong.

Bibliography

ALEXANDER, R. J. (1984) *Primary Teaching*, Eastbourne, Holt Education.

ARMSTRONG, M. (1980) *Closely Observed Children*, London, Writer and Readers.

ASE, ATM, MA, NATE (1989) *The national curriculum, making it work for the primary school*, Hatfield, Association for Science Education.

ASHTON, P. M. E., Kneen, P., Davies, F. and Holly, B. J. (1975) *Aims of Primary Education: A Study of Teachers' Opinions*, London, University of London Press.

AULD, R. (1979) *William Tyndale Junior and Infant Schools: Public Enquiry*, London, ILEA.

AUSUBEL, D. P., NOVAK, J. D. and HANESIAN, H. (1978) *Educational Psychology: A Cognitive View*, New York, Rinehart and Winston.

BENNETT, N. and DESFORGES, C. (1984) *Quality of Pupil Learning Experiences*, Hove, Erlbaum (Lawrence) Associates Ltd.

BLACKIE, J. (1982) The Open University, *Approaches to Evaluation*, E364, Block 2, Part 3, Milton Keynes, The Open University Press.

BLENKIN, G. M. and KELLY, A. V. (Eds) (1983) *The Primary Curriculum in Action*, Chapter 1, London, Harper and Row.

BLYTH, W. A. L., COOPER, K. R., DERRICOT, R., ELLIOTT, G., SUMNER, H. and WAPLINGTON, A. (1976) *Place, Time and Society 8-13: Curriculum Planning in History, Geography and Social Science*, Glasgow and Bristol, Colins/ESL.

BOARD OF EDUCATION (1931) *Report of the Consultative Committee on The Primary School*, (Hadow Report), Chairman Sir W. H. Hadow, CBE, London, HMSO.

BRIERLEY, J. (1978) *Growing and Learning*, London, Ward Lock Educational.

BURSTALL, C., JAMIESON, M., COHEN, S. and HARGREAVES, M. (1974) *Primary French in the Balance*, Slough, NFER.

CLAPARÈDE, E. (1960) in preface to PIAGET, J. *The Language and Thought of the Child*, London, Routledge and Kegan Paul.

CLIFT, P. S., WEINER, G. G. and WILSON, E. L. (1981) *Record Keeping in Primary Schools*, London, Macmillan.

COCKERILL, G. *The Middle Years*, in PLASKOW, M. (1985) *Life and Death of the Schools Council, op. cit.*

COX, C. B. and DYSON, A. E. (Eds) (1969–1977) *Black Papers*, London, The Critical Quarterly Society.

DES (1967) *Children and their Primary Schools, A report of Central Advisory Council for Education (England)*, (Plowden Report) Chairman Lady B Plowden, London, HMSO (2 vols).

DES (1972) Cmnd. 5174 *Education: A Framework for Expansion* London, HMSO.

DES (1975) Cmnd. 5720, London, HMSO.

DES (1975) *A language for life*, (Bullock Report) Committee of Inquiry, Chairman Sir Alan Bullock, London, HMSO.

DES (1977) *Educating Our Children, Four Subjects for Debate*, London, DES.

DES (1977) Cmnd. 6869 (1977) *Education in Schools, A Consultative Document*, London, HMSO.

DES (1977) *A New Partnership for Our Schools*, Committee of Inquiry chaired by Thomas Taylor, London, HMSO.

DES (1978) Cmnd. 7212 *Special Educational Needs, Report of the Committee of Inquiry into the Education of Handicapped Children and Young People*, Chairman, H. M. Warnock, London, HMSO.

DES (1979) *Local Authority Arrangements for the School Curriculum*, London, HMSO.

DES (1981) *Circular 6/81*, London, HMSO.

DES (1981) Cmnd. 8273 *West Indian Children in Our Schools*, Interim Report of the Committee of Inquiry into the Education of Children from Minority Ethnic Groups, Chairman M. A. Rampton, London, HMSO.

DES (1982) *Mathematics Counts*, (Cockroft Report), Committee of Inquiry chaired by Dr W. H. Cockroft, London, HMSO.

DES (1983) Cmnd. 8836 *Teaching Quality*, London, HMSO.

DES (1985) Cmnd. 9469 *Better Schools*, London, HMSO.

DES (1985) Cmnd. 9453 *Education for All*, Final Report of the Committee of Inquiry into the Education of Children from Minority Ethnic Groups, Chairman Lord Swann, London, HMSO.

DES (1986) *Local Authority Policies for the School Curriculum, Report on the Circular 8/83 Review*, London, HMSO.

DES (1986) *Educational Statistical Bulletin 6/86*, London, HMSO.

DES (1988) Press Notice 179/88, London, DES.

DES (1989) *The National Curriculum: From Policy to Practice*, London, HMSO.

DES/APU (1981) *Mathematical Development, Primary Survey Report No. 2*, London, HMSO.

DES/APU (1982) *Language Performance in Schools: Primary Survey Report No. 2*, London, HMSO.

DES/APU (1983) *Science Report for Teachers: 1, Science at Age 11*, London, HMSO.

DES/APU (1985) Memorandum submitted to the HOUSE OF COMMONS EDUCATION, SCIENCE AND ARTS COMMITTEE, see *Achievement in Primary Schools*, Minutes of Evidence, Session 1984–85, HC 48, p. 320, London, HMSO.

Desforges, C. (1984) *Understanding the quality of pupil learning experience*, in Entwhistle, N. (Ed.) *New Directions in Educational Psychology I: Learning and Teaching*, Lewes, Falmer Press.

DES/HMI (1978) *Primary Education in England*, London, HMSO.

DES/HMI (1980) *Matters for Discussion, A View of the Curriculum*, London, HMSO.

DES/HMI (1982) *The New Teacher in School*, London, HMSO.

DES/HMI (1982) *Education 5–9: An Illustrative Survey of 80 First Schools in England*, London, HMSO.

DES/HMI (1985) *Education 8–12 in Combined and Middle Schools*, London, HMSO.

DES/HMI (1985) *The Curriculum from 5 to 16, Curriculum Matters 2*, London, HMSO.

DES/HMI (1989) *Aspects of Primary Education, The Teaching and Learning of Mathematics*, London, HMSO.

DES/WO (1977) Cmnd. 6869, London, HMSO.

DES/WO (1977) *A Study of School Building*, London, HMSO.

DES/WO (1980) *A Framework for the School Curriculum*, London, HMSO.

DES/WO (1981) *The School Curriculum*, London, HMSO.

DES/WO (1985) *Better Schools*, London, HMSO.

DES/WO (1985) *Science 5–16: A statement of policy*, London and Cardiff, DES and Welsh Office.

DES/WO (1987) *The National Curriculum 5–16, a consultation document*, London, DES.

DES/WO (1988) *National Curriculum, Task Group on Assessment and Testing: a Report*, London, HMSO.

DES/WO (1988) *Task Group on Assessment and Testing Report, A Digest for Schools*, reports of committee chaired by Paul Black, London, HMSO.

DES/WO (1988) *English for Ages 5 to 11*, Subject Working Party chaired by C. B. Cox, London, HMSO.

DONALDSON, M. (1978) *Children's Minds*, London, Fontana.

EDUCATION REFORM ACT (1988) London, HMSO.

ENNEVER, L. and HARLEN, W. (1972) *With Objectives in Mind: Guide to Science 5-13*, London, MacDonald Educational.

FROOME, S. H. (1969) *The Mystique of Modern Maths* in COX, C. B. and DYSON, A. E. (Eds) *Black Paper 2, op. cit.*

GALTON, M. and SIMON, B. (Eds) (1980) *Progress and Performance in the Primary Classroom*, London, Routledge and Kegan Paul.

GALTON, M., SIMON, B. and CROLL, P. (1980) *Inside the Primary Classroom*, London, Routledge and Kegan Paul.

GIPPS, C. (1983) *Testing Children: standardised testing in local education authorities and schools*, Oxford, Heinemann Educational.

GIPPS, C. and WOOD, R. (1981) *The Testing of Reading in LEAs: the Bullock Report seven years on*, in *Educational Studies*, Vol. 7, No. 2, Abingdon, Carfax Publishing Co..

GOLDSTEIN, H. and NUTTALL, D. (4 July 1989) *Education Guardian: Screen Tests for Progress*, London, Guardian Newspapers.

GORMAN, T. (1986) *The Framework for the Assessment of Language*, DES/APU, Windsor, NFER-Nelson.

GRAY, J. and SATTERLEY, D. (1981) *Formal or Informal? A reassessment of the British evidence* 51, 2, pp. 190–193, British Journal of Educational Psychology.

HALSEY, A. (Ed.) (1972) *Educational Priority, Volume 1: E.P.A. Problems and Policies*, London, HMSO.

HALSEY, P. H. (1989): Letter dated 13th July from the Chairman and Chief Executive of the School Examinations and Assessment Council to the Secretary of State, reference MRF/PUB6/1.

HAVILAND, J. (1988) *Take Care, Mr Baker!*, London, Fourth Estate.

HIRST, P. H. and PETERS, R. S. (1970) *The Logic of Education*, London, Routledge and Kegan Paul.

HIRST, P. H. (1974) *Knowledge and the Curriculum*, London, Routledge and Kegan Paul.

HOHMANN, M., BANET, B. and WEIKART, D. P. (1979) *Young Children in Action*, Ypsilanti, Michigan, The High/Scope Press.

HOUSE OF COMMONS EDUCATION, SCIENCE AND ARTS COMMITTEE (1986) *Achievement in Primary Schools*, Third Report, Session 1985–86: HC 40–I, Volume 1, London, HMSO.

HOUSE OF COMMONS EDUCATION, SCIENCE AND ARTS COMMITTEE (1989) *Educational Provision for the Under Fives*, First Report, Volume 1, Session 1988–89, 30–I, London, HMSO.

ILEA (1985) *Improving Primary Schools, Report of Committee on Primary Education*, chaired by Norman Thomas, London, ILEA.

JOSEPH, Sir Keith, Secretary of State for Education and Science (6 January 1984): speech to the North of England Conference, Sheffield.

LAWTON, D. (1986) *Curriculum and Assessment* in RANSON, S. and TOMLINSON, J. (Eds) (1986) *The Changing Government of Education*, *op. cit.*

MACKAY, D. (1969 and following) *Breakthrough to Literacy*, London, Longman.

MACLURE, M. and HARGREAVES, M. (1986) *Speaking and Listening, Assessment at Age 11*, Windsor, APU/NFER-Nelson.

MATTHEWS, G. (1967) *I do and I understand*, Edinburgh, Chambers.

MORTIMORE, P., SAMMONS, P., STOLL, L., LEWIS, D. and ECOB, R. (1988) *School Matters, The Junior Years*, Wells, Open Book Publishers.

NORTHAMPTONSHIRE LEA (1983) *Principles for the Primary Curriculum*, Northampton, Northamptonshire County Council.

NORTHAMPTONSHIRE LEA (1985) *The School Curriculum. A Framework of Principles*, Northampton, Northamptonshire County Council.

PLASKOW, M. (Ed.) (1985) *Life and Death of the Schools Council*, Lewes, The Falmer Press.

RANSON, S. and TOMLINSON, J. (Eds) (1986) *The Changing Government of Education*, London, Allen and Unwin.

ROWLAND, S. (1984) *The Enquiring Classroom*, Lewes, The Falmer Press.

RUDDOCK, G. (1988) *Diagnostic Testing and Primary Mathematics*, in *Issues in Primary Education: Recent Research*, produced for NFER Members' Conference, Slough, NFER.

RUTTER, M., MAUGHAM, B., MORTIMORE, P. and OUSTON, J. (1979) *Fifteen Thousand Hours*, London, Open Books.

SCHOOLS COUNCIL WORKING PAPER 70 (1981) *The Practical Curriculum*, London, Methuen Educational.

SCHOOLS COUNCIL (1983) *Primary Practice*, London, Methuen.

SCHOOLS CURRICULUM DEVELOPMENT COMMITTEE (1989) *The National Writing Project*, materials to be published by Thomas Nelson, Walton on Thames.

SHIPMAN, M. (1983) *Assessment in Primary and Middle Schools*, London, Croom Helm.

SIMON, B. (1980) *Inside the Primary Classroom*, 22, 3, pp. 68ff., *Forum*, Leicester, PSW (Educational) Publications.

SIMPSON, E. (1986) *The Department of Education and Science*, in RANSON, S. and TOMLINSON, J. (Eds) *The Changing Government of Education*, *op. cit.*

SMITH, D. and TOMLINSON, S. (1989) *The School Effect: A Study of Multi-Racial Comprehensives*, London, Policy Studies Institute.

STUART, K. B. and WELLS, B. K. (1972) *The Trend of Reading Standards*, Slough, NFER.

STATHAM, J., MACKINNON, D. and CATHCART, H. (1989) *The Education Factfile*, London, Hodder and Stoughton.

STONE, A. L. (1949) *The Story of a School*, Ministry of Education, London, HMSO.

TIZARD, B. and HUGHES, M. (1984) *Young children learning, talking and thinking at home and at school*, London, Fontana.

TOUGH, J. (1977) *Talking and Learning: A Guide to Fostering Communication Skills in Nursery and Infant Schools*, London, Ward Lock.

UNSTEAD, R. J. (1955) *Looking at History*, London, A. and C. Black.

WARNOCK, H. M. (1978) *Meeting Special Educational Needs*, London, HMSO.

WASTNEDGE, E. R. (Ed.) (1967) *Nuffield Junior Science, Teachers' Guide*, London, Collins.

WHITE, J. (1986) *The Assessment of Writing*, Windsor, APU/NFER-Nelson.

Index

Index